THE S.A.L.T. PLAN

HOW TO PREPARE FOR AN ECONOMIC CRISIS OF BIBLICAL PROPORTIONS

CHUCK BENTLEY

YOU ARE THE SALT OF THE EARTH.
BUT IF THE SALT LOSES ITS SALTINESS,
HOW CAN IT BE MADE SALTY AGAIN?
IT IS NO LONGER GOOD FOR ANYTHING, EXCEPT
TO BE THROWN OUT AND TRAMPLED BY MEN.

- Matthew 5:13

The S.A.L.T. Plan is a trademark of Crown Financial Ministries, Inc.

ISBN: 978-1-56427-299-7

Cover Design: Sean Allen
Interior Art and Layout Design: Sean Allen
Editor: Jim Henry

This book contains quotes from various individuals and references to a broad range of source materials. Any such mentions should not be viewed as an endorsement of the overall theological or political views of any particular person, nor (unless otherwise noted) as a recommendation of any particular book, article or website.

Please note: *The S.A.L.T. Plan*™ is designed to serve you with general guidelines and suggestions. It should not be used in a strict manner. You should employ all available resources you deem necessary for your unique financial situation, including professional financial planning and investment advisors who share your biblical worldview.

Printed in the U.S.A.

December 2011 Edition

I dedicate this book to you, God's humble servant who lives for His glory and looks not only to your own interests but to the interests of others. You shine like stars in the universe.

Thank you to our team at Crown that made this book possible. Jim Henry, Megan Pacheco, Sheila Thompson and Robert Dickie III.

CONTENTS

INTRODUCTION
Something's Happening Here

The idea of preparing for hardship is timeless.

Noah built an ark. Joseph stored up grain. Moses and the Israelites stocked up before heading off into the wilderness.

The truth is, we never really know when tough times or calamity will strike, so God, in His infinite mercy and wisdom, has warned us to be prepared.

"The prudent see danger and take refuge, but the simple keep going and suffer for it." [1]

The dismal state of the world economy is certainly reason enough to act now, but it should not be the only reason to prepare for difficult times. Even if your country's economy recovers, that doesn't insulate you, as an individual, from the danger of a severe financial setback.

My personal observation is that as a people, we are woefully unprepared for what lies ahead. I believe it is time to prepare but not to be paranoid. In fact, being prepared should dramatically reduce or eliminate fears about the uncertain future we all must face.

Our extensive periods of peace and comfort have caused us not only to be out of shape for trials and testing but to be unwilling

[1] Proverbs 27:12

to admit that conditioning for such an event is even necessary. Like an aged athlete, we often think of what we were once capable of achieving long after we've stopped doing even the basics of working out or staying in condition for strenuous competitions.

Now, I'm not saying it's the end of the world—quite the contrary. Based on Jesus' own words, I've always believed that anyone who tries to set the date will be wrong, *"...because the Son of Man will come at an hour when you do not expect him."* [2]

Apart from the occasional Hollywood movie fantasy, the mainstream media rarely concerns itself with biblical concepts such as the end times. However, when newspaper headlines begin to ask—"What Time is it?" "Do Disasters, Wars Signal the End?" "Are We Prepared for Disaster?"—you have to wonder, if it's not the end times, just what time is it, anyway?

Putting the question another way, what has the pop culture types so spooked? We've always had wars and rumors of wars. We've always had hurricanes and tsunamis and earthquakes. We've had massively destructive volcanoes and even the odd meteor or two. So what's different about now? Why is the world starting to wonder if (some) believers are on to something with this "end times" business?

I believe a general sense of dread is beginning to form in the secular culture and, yes, even in the Body of Christ. And why wouldn't it?

- **Economies everywhere are on the verge of collapse.**

- **9-11 showed us that no country and no people are immune from Islamic terrorism.**

- **A few years ago, we were told there was a giant hole in**

---

[2] Matthew 24:44

the ozone layer and we were all going to fry.

· More recently, images of polar bears lazing on ice drifts were used to warn us that the oceans were rising and we were all going to drown.

By the way, if you're still panicking over global warming, don't worry; the latest climatic revelation is that another *Ice Age* [3] is coming. Stock up on sunscreen or mukluks—your choice!

I am not one of those "doom and gloom" types. I am not a conspiracy theorist. I am not a prophet. I am not a pessimist. Generally, I try to remain optimistic—with good reason. As a believer, I know that the sovereign God of the universe is still on the throne and in charge. All who have read ahead in the Bible know that in the end, we win!

Psalm 112 assures us, *"...Blessed is the man who fears the Lord, who finds great delight in His commands...He will have no fear of bad news; his heart is steadfast, trusting in the Lord."*

However, like the Bible, I am a realist.

We don't need the End Times to arrive before we could experience severe interruptions in the systems and infrastructure that we all take for granted—energy, transportation, food production and health care to name a few.

We have no control over the global supply of petroleum—the lifeblood of industry. At any time, drought, floods or some other weather-related disaster could take a season's harvest—or two, or three. A new disease could emerge that is beyond our current medical technologies to cure.

---

[3] The UK Register, "Earth May Be Headed into a Mini Ice Age Within a Decade: Physicists Say Sunspot Cycle Is 'Going into Hibernation,'" June 14, 2011. (http://www.theregister.co.uk/2011/06/14/ice_age/)

While those scenarios may be hypothetical, our economic difficulties are all too real. We likely will recover from our immediate woes—for a time. But it is difficult to envision fundamental changes taking place that would ensure the long term viability of western economies. We have become addicted to debt—as people and as nations. If that addiction doesn't cause a worldwide financial collapse, it will at the least severely curtail our current affluent lifestyle—more likely sooner than later. While public debt is mounting at prodigious rates in Europe and the U.S., governments are on the hook for trillions of dollars more in unfunded entitlement benefits that the people will demand in the not too distant future. Most economists believe that if the western economies collapse, so will go the world.

I'm not saying that disaster will strike today, next year, or even in a decade. As I said, I'm not a prophet; but we do have God's Word that instructs us to be *"prudent see danger and take refuge."* The simple (foolish) do nothing and suffer for it.

Over 35 years ago, our late founder, Larry Burkett, warned of the dangers of a pending economic crisis.

"Isolating the economy from any other event, a prudent observer would say that we have a problem. Notice that the United States' economy and most of the world's economy is unstable.

· The value of the US dollar is shrinking on the world market.

· Inflation is growing, while real production has dropped off.

· The trend toward economic collapse – where inflation runs away and is followed by a major depression – seems irreversible.

- **Politicians make decisions based on what is popular rather than financially sound.**

- **Rather than working on a feasible solution to our problems, government officials quibble about which support group should get the most handouts.**

- **Most families live on the brink of disaster. The excessive use of personal and business credit has weakened the already shaky family structure."**

> — Larry Burkett,
> *Your Finances in Changing Times,* 1975

Larry picked up on this theme in greater detail in 1991 with his bestseller, *The Coming Economic Earthquake.* And today, we find ourselves in the midst of the greatest economic crisis since the Great Depression and possibly in history.

So, to answer that glaring newspaper headline, "What Time Is It?"—I believe a tectonic shift is underway—a shift in the balance of social and economic power that will mark the 21st century as an era of massive change at the very foundational levels of the world as we know it.

This shift is easily visible to the prudent and clearly indicates that it's time to *prepare.*

Will an economic disaster of biblical proportions occur in our generation? No man knows. But we can state with certainty that it is *possible.*

Look at these headlines from highly regarded sources and you can understand why I see an ever increasing risk of an epic financial event occurring:

"FOR THE FIRST TIME IN RECORDED HISTORY, no fewer than five major Western nations—Portugal, Ireland, Italy, Greece and Spain—are now edging towards default. Nobody knows precisely when the first default will be announced, and the first shoe could drop at virtually any moment."

-DR. MARTIN WEISS,
Chairman, Weiss Group, Inc. [4]

"THE GOVERNMENTS WORLDWIDE (I DON'T PAY MUCH ATTENTION TO ECONOMISTS) want us to believe that the worst is behind us because the financial system is built upon the foundation of trust and confidence. Both of these were battered badly when it was shown that much of the world's prosperity over the past few decades was simply a mirage that, once dispersed, left behind only debt with no means of future production. Now they want us to believe that they fixed the problem via more debt.

"What I will be watching for this year is sovereign and U.S. municipal debt corpses floating to the surface sometime in the months ahead."

-STEVE HENNINGSEN, Chief Investment Strategist and partner, The Wealth Conservancy in Boulder, CO [5]

"NO, THE WORST IS YET TO COME. No structural changes have been made, no problems have been fixed. Printing money, a.k.a.

---

[4] Physicists Say Sunspot Cycle Is 'Going into Hibernation,'" June 14, 2011. (http://www.theregister.co.uk/2011/06/14/ice_age/)

[5] Jeff Clark, "'Investment Legends: '"Dollar Collapse Inevitable,'" Casey Research, March 23, 2011, http://www.caseyresearch.com/articles/investment-legends

Quantitative Easing, is a quick fix that has postponed the problem, yet also made it a lot worse. I would say that we are still in the early stages of the crisis and have another 4-8 years to go."

- DR. KRASSIMIR PETROV,
Austrian economist, Ph.D. Economics,
Ohio State University [6]

"THE DEBT PROBLEMS FACING ADVANCED ECONOMIES ARE EVEN WORSE THAN WE THOUGHT. The basic facts are that combined debt in the rich club has risen from 165pc of GDP thirty years ago to 310pc today, led by Japan at 456pc and Portugal at 363pc. Debt is rising to points that are above anything we have seen, except during major wars. Public debt ratios are currently on an explosive path in a number of countries. These countries will need to implement drastic policy changes. Stabilization might not be enough."

-STEPHEN CECCHETTI,
Bank for International Settlements [7]

While government officials in the U.S. and Europe continue to tell us that our economic troubles are manageable, independent sources are hardly convinced. If you spend any time reading financial columns and blogs, you soon discover that there is no end to frightening predictions and negative outlooks. There is plenty of fear to go around right now.

We need to be ready for big changes that seem imminent, even if they never materialize. No one who is caught unprepared will be able to say he was not warned. These problems have been developing over a number of decades and as my grandfather liked to say: "Nobody should get run over by a slow-moving train."

---

[6] Ibid.

[7] Stephen Cecchetti, quoted in Ambrose Evans-Pritchard, "When Debt Levels Turn Cancerous" *The UK Telegraph*, Aug. 31, 2011, http://blogs.telegraph.co.uk/finance/ambroseevans-pritchard/100011744/when-debt-levels-turn-cancerous/

In the chapters ahead, I will share a plan to help prepare you financially and spiritually by looking to God's Word for advice and wisdom. We call it The S.A.L.T. Plan™ for reasons which will become obvious.

I need to make one more point perfectly clear. This is not a self-reliance survival guide. My purpose is not to help you stock up on guns, gold and grain so that you can "hunker in the bunker," separated and safe from a world that is hurting.

I want you to weather the coming storms, yes, but to do it as "the salt of the earth," as Jesus has directed us.

We are to be God's *preserving* agents filled with love in our hearts and surplus resources that we can share with others who are suffering.

Just as strongly as I believe there is trouble coming, I also know that it will be the greatest opportunity for demonstrating the love of Christ and sharing the Gospel that we will see in our lifetimes. This financial and spiritual preparation will enable you to be the compassionate representative of Christ's interests during a time of need.

"For I was hungry and you gave me something to eat, I was thirsty and you gave me something to drink, I was a stranger and you invited me in, I needed clothes and you clothed me, I was sick and you looked after me, I was in prison and you came to visit me." [8]

So before we get to the actual preparation, we need to get some idea of what we may be facing in the future, which I lay out in Part One, The Four Scenarios.

---

[8] Matthew 25:35-36

Then we'll dive deep in Scripture to see how God's people have handled similar challenges in the past in Part Two, The Four Famines.

And finally, with a firm understanding of where we've been and what may lie ahead, we'll prepare for the future as God's people in Part Three, The S.A.L.T. Plan™.

PART 1 ONE

WHAT THE FUTURE MAY HOLD

"Do not boast about tomorrow, for you do not know what a day may bring forth."

~ PROVERBS 27:1

The Four Economic Scenarios

DELEVERAGE & DIVISION

BAILOUT UNTIL COLLAPSE

GROWTH FUELED RETURN TO NORMALCY

UNIFICATION & NEW WORLD ORDER

CHAPTER ONE

A HOUSE BUILT
UPON THE SAND?

Nowhere in the Bible is debt ever described in positive terms. God's Word consistently tells us that debt is something to be avoided whenever and wherever possible.

That principle which tells us to fear falling into debt applies to individuals, businesses and government at all levels.

The United States and the European Union are up to their respective necks in red ink. Meanwhile, the People's Republic of China, an unapologetic communist nation, is swimming in cash. Worse, China holds much of the public debt of the United States. Put another way, they are the lender the Bible calls the master, we are the slave.

Deuteronomy 28

Let's apply a biblical lens to the image of the map with the following verses:

"If you fully obey the Lord your God and carefully follow all his commands I give you today, the Lord your God will set you high above all the nations on earth. All these blessings will come on you and accompany you if you obey the Lord your God" [1]

"The Lord will grant you abundant prosperity—in the fruit of your womb, the young of your livestock and the crops of your ground—in the land he swore to your ancestors to give you.

"The Lord will open the heavens, the storehouse of his bounty, to send rain on your land in season and to bless all the work of your hands. You will lend to many nations but will borrow from none. The Lord will make you the head, not the tail. If you pay attention to the commands of the Lord your God that I give you this day and carefully follow them, you will always be at the top, never at the bottom. [2]

[1] Deuteronomy 28:1-2
[2] Deuteronomy 28:11-13

"However, if you do not obey the Lord your God and do not carefully follow all his commands and decrees I am giving you today, all these curses will come on you and overtake you.... [3]

"The foreigners who reside among you will rise above you higher and higher, but you will sink lower and lower. They will lend to you, but you will not lend to them. They will be the head, but you will be the tail...." [4]

So, through this lens, we can plainly see a move away from obedience to God and His financial principles and towards reliance upon debt. The result is that the United States and Europe have moved from their lofty position at the head of lending nations to the tail of borrowing nations.

While economists point fingers at federal deficits, trade imbalances, globalization, job loss or any number of isolated symptoms, I believe we are at a breaking point in a huge economic cycle that calls for a greater change than simply tweaking economic policy or financial behaviors.

Forgetting God

Phillip Yancey describes the cyclical relationship between discipline and decadence that could not be more relevant to our economic problems:

> "Gordon Cosby, the founding pastor of Church of the Savior in Washington, D.C....noted that high-commitment Christian communities begin with a strong sense of devotion, which expresses itself in a life of discipline. Groups organized around devotion and discipline tend to produce abundance, but ultimately that very success breaks down discipline and leads to decadence.

[3] Deuteronomy 28:15
[4] Deuteronomy 28:43-44

"Cosby termed this pattern the 'monastic cycle'—with good reason...In the sixth century, early Benedictines worked hard to clear forests and cultivate land, investing their surplus in drainage, livestock, and seed. Six centuries later, according to historian Paul Johnson, 'Benedictine abbeys had virtually ceased to be spiritual institutions. They had become collegiate sinecures reserved very largely for members of the upper classes.' The abbots absorbed about half the order's revenue in order to maintain their luxurious lifestyles, becoming 'unenterprising, upper-class parasites...'

"Perhaps we should call this trend the 'human cycle' rather than the 'monastic cycle,' because it applies to individuals as well as to religious movements and nations. Beginning with Adam and Eve's brief sojourn in Paradise, people have shown an inability to handle prosperity. We turn to God out of need and forget God when things go well." [5]

As Yancey points out, this is more than a "monastic cycle." it can be used to explain the macro-economic cycles of nations, as well.

You need only glance at this cycle to see where both Europe and the United States are headed today.

---

[5] Philip Yancey, "Forgetting God: Why Decadence Drives Out Discipline," *Christianity Today*, Sept. 1, 2004. http://www.christianitytoday.com/ct/2004/september/21.104.html

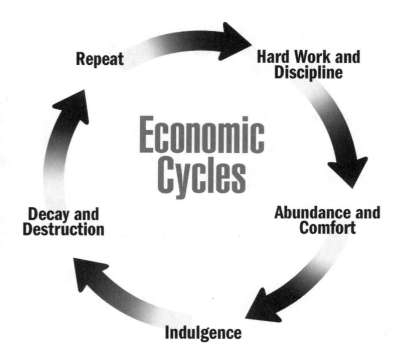

So Where Is the Hope?

It was Larry Burkett's hope, and I share it today, that we understand the very fragile economy that surrounds us, see the danger we are facing and take action. God's Word repeatedly warns us to be prepared for storms of every kind.

A great example of this is found in the parable of The Wise and Foolish Builders.

"Therefore everyone who hears these words of mine and puts them into practice is like a wise man who built his house on the

rock. The rain came down, the streams rose, and the winds blew and beat against that house; yet it did not fall, because it had its foundation on the rock. But everyone who hears these words of mine and does not put them into practice is like a foolish man who built his house on sand. The rain came down, the streams rose, a nd the winds blew and beat against that house, and it fell with a great crash." [6]

Notice two things about this parable: First, both houses get the same storm; both the wise and the foolish will experience trials. Secondly, the wise builder must do more than hear God's Word; he must put them into practice.

Our true hope should not be in a recovery, but a revival. A revival is a sincere turning back to God's ways and wholeheartedly embracing our personal need for Him.

As we move from what is certainly the point of indulgence on our macro-economic cycle toward what appears to be decay and destruction, I want to share with you four possible outcomes.

[6] Matthew 7:24-27

CHAPTER TWO
2

THE SCENARIOS DEFINED

Many economists believe we will see one of the following four scenarios in the coming years. It is also possible that we will experience elements of two or more scenarios to varying degrees. For example, a nation may elect to engage in a partial austerity program accompanied by policies that stimulate economic growth.

The scenarios are given in their pure forms here so that we can define terms and more easily grasp the concepts involved. As such, they are not complicated.

Scenario One

DELEVERAGE & DIVISION

Deleveraging simply means to pay down one's debt. In the case of public debt, deleveraging requires a government to reduce spending on social entitlement programs and redirect revenues toward debt reduction—also known as "austerity."

The possibility exists that corrective measures to deleverage the massive debts in the Eurozone will lead to the breakup of the now economically consolidated nations. Should the austerity plan fail and Greece default on its debt, it will be difficult to contain the ripple effect. This event, though once thought to be highly unlikely, would have significant negative consequences according to experts, including sovereign and corporate default, and the collapse of the European banking system and international trade disruptions.

While this scenario looks bleak, I prefer that economically weak nations be allowed to fail and start over than to have stronger countries continue to attempt to bail them out.

Scenario Two

BAILOUT UNTIL COLLAPSE

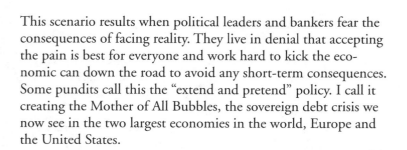

This scenario results when political leaders and bankers fear the consequences of facing reality. They live in denial that accepting the pain is best for everyone and work hard to kick the economic can down the road to avoid any short-term consequences. Some pundits call this the "extend and pretend" policy. I call it creating the Mother of All Bubbles, the sovereign debt crisis we now see in the two largest economies in the world, Europe and the United States.

This scenario has far more devastating consequences than deleverage and division. David Galland of Casey Research writes that recent statements by former Federal Reserve Chairman Alan Greenspan and Obama economic advisor Larry Summers that the U.S. would never default on its debts as long as it can print money and borrow deny the real danger:

"Of course, Greenspan and Summers were referring to an overt default—of just not paying—and not to a covert default engineered by inflation. Unfortunately, like virtually all of the power elite, both

miss the point that the mountain of debt that has been heaped up since 1971 is fast reaching the point of collapsing like a too-big tailings pile and taking the monetary system down with it."[1]

Scenario Three

GROWTH FUELED RETURN TO NORMALCY

This scenario is for optimists, and I certainly hope it eventually wins out. It is still possible that the United States will reverse course and kick into a long and steady period of economic growth. This would avert a significant period of recession and pave the way for increases in jobs, wages, real estate values and corporate growth. That, in turn, would provide needed tax revenues to end our nation's wildly out-of-control deficit spending and debt accumulation.

John Mauldin, a widely read market analyst, takes this position. He believes our political leaders "get it"—they see the potential for a global disaster and thus will take the corrective action necessary to keep the train on the tracks.

John is not alone in this assessment; many very bright investors

[1] http://www.johnmauldin.com/outsidethebox/is-the-us-monetary-system-on-the-verge-of-collapseDavid Galland, "Is the US Monetary System on the Verge of Collapse?" Casey Research, Sept. 20, 2011. http://www.caseyresearch.com/articles/us-monetary-system-verge-collapse

also believe we are now on this path. I sincerely hope they're right, but I'm not so optimistic. You can follow John's analysis at johnmauldin.com, and I'll leave it to him to make his case.

Scenario Four

UNIFICATION & NEW WORLD ORDER

I must again insert a disclaimer here that I am neither a conspiracy theorist nor a prophet. However, I do keep up with world events, and there is some evidence that unification of the world's economic superpowers is at least a remote possibility.

Since coming to the brink of a worldwide financial meltdown in 2008, many leaders, including members of the G 20, have called for new rules to govern the global economy. A 2009 Reuters article revealed that the groundwork is being laid for a more unified global economy.

"The Group of 20 is set to become the premier coordinating body on global economic issues, reflecting a new world economic order in which emerging market countries like China are much more relevant...By making the G20 the new global economic coordina-

tor, countries are committing to maintaining cooperation even after the global financial upheaval and recession recede." [2]

The growing influence of the Group of 20 makes it at least plausible that through this new world "economic order," much of the globe could be controlled without a unified government or political structure in place. The Eurozone is a pilot project for economic interdependence without political union.

A Biblical Focus

We don't know which of these scenarios will play out in our future. We do know, however, that God's Word is a sure guide for every economic scenario. It covers all contingencies. The good news is that Christians can do well in any economic circumstance. To do well means to be a good and faithful steward of the resources God entrusts to you; to be prudent and watchful. That is our part; He is responsible for the results.

For Christians, this means we must filter out the ungodly advice that competes for our minds. We must be able to discern the narrow path of God's ways, ignoring the broader path of the world.

From the parable of the Wise and Foolish Builders, it is obvious that doing well means building your house upon the rock, not sand. But who or what are the rock and the sand? Contrary to popular belief, the rock is not your bank account. If you imagine that God only spares those who have a large stockpile of resources, you would be wrong. The rock in this parable is Christ, of course, and the sand is anything else—a big salary, high net worth, or a leveraged lifestyle.

[2] Lesley Wroughten, "SNAP ANALYSIS: New World Economic Order Takes Shape at G20," Reuters, Sept. 25, 2009. http://www.reuters.com/article/2009/09/25/us-g20-imf-snapanalysis-sb-idUSTRE58O1FB20090925

God is not against planning or wise financial moves, but doing well in any economy means keeping your heart faithful to serve God, even in the midst of crisis. Too much emphasis, even by Christians, is placed upon financial success. It's causing a great deal of needless worry and stress.

So let's go into God's Word to see how others prepared for an economic event of biblical proportions.

PART 2 TWO

LESSONS FROM THE PAST

*"The fear of the Lord is the beginning
of knowledge, but fools despise
wisdom and discipline."*

~ Proverbs 1:7

CHAPTER THREE

JOSEPH AND THE FIRST GREAT FAMINE

The 4 Famines

GENESIS 41

Famine:	Egypt
God's Servant:	Joseph
Attributes:	Save

1 KINGS 18

Famine:	Israel
God's Servant:	Elijah
Attributes:	Serve God

2 KINGS 6-7

Famine:	Famine/War
God's Servant:	Elisha
Attributes:	End Self-Reliance

ACTS 11

Famine:	Early Church
God's Servant:	Agabus
Attributes:	Serve Others

Famine - An Economic Event

As I've studied Scripture, it has become clear to me that when God's people go through times of terrible suffering, it's usually the result of one of three calamities: famine, war or plague. I know this sounds harsh, but if you have to rank them in order of pain, famine probably involves the least suffering—depending, of course, on its duration. War is hideous; plagues are hideous. When they strike, death is certain. Once begun, they ravage out of control. Famine, on the other hand, can be managed to some degree.

How then, might we envision famine occurring in present times? I believe the lessons we learn from Biblical famines provide valuable insights that we need to prepare for a widespread economic collapse. Certainly, such an event would be accompanied by severe interruptions in food production and distribution.

Throughout history, famine has been one of the gentler ways the Lord has disciplined His people and gotten their attention. God uses times of trouble to help us draw near to Him, that we might call out for His help.

If we naturally turn to God in our pain, what about when times are good?

I think you know the answer to that one—we just as naturally turn away from the God who loves us when we foolishly begin to believe we no longer need Him. The very affluence of Western Civilization, once built on the foundation of God's principles, has caused us to forget about the One who made it all possible. We simply forget God when we're comfortable. That's the human tendency. What then, might be God's response?

Throughout the Old Testament, God used pain and suffering to correct His people when they had gone astray. Why would we,

His people today, expect anything different? I believe we must anticipate and prepare for that discipline. I believe it is coming.

The first famine recorded in Scripture is found in Genesis 12. Abram left his country and traveled to Egypt to escape famine. Then, as now, one had to be prepared to travel in the event of a catastrophe like famine. In present times, could we not equate famine to job loss? After all, a famine in Abram's time was an economic event, as well.

Are you prepared to move to another location if no work is available in your area? Such a move requires more than suffering the pain of leaving family and friends behind. It takes *money*. So as we explore several famines of the Old Testament, think of them as biblical *economic events*.

Brother, Can You Spare a Cup of Grain?

The first truly great famine recorded in Scripture was far more severe than the one experienced by Abram. In Genesis 41, we see that the Pharaoh of Egypt dreamed of seven years of plenty followed by seven years of famine. He placed Joseph in charge of his Kingdom with the mission to save it. Joseph immediately put an emergency plan into effect, confiscating all of the grain and giving the people only what they needed to survive. By this action, he accumulated a vast amount of grain, locked up in Pharaoh's storehouses.

Later, in Genesis 47, when the seven years of famine began, the people of Canaan were forced to journey to Egypt and submit themselves to Pharaoh in order to survive. They had heard of the huge amount of grain that Joseph put in storage. He literally had the lives of the people of Egypt and Canaan in his hands at that point, since he'd confiscated all of the grain. Keep in mind that this radical move and those that followed were intended to save the people, not to gain their possessions.

As the famine continued, Joseph knew that taking the grain would not be enough. In exchange for the grain needed just to keep the people alive, he then collected their money—all of it. You get an idea of how serious this famine was, since there was surprisingly little grumbling. Can you imagine the people's reaction if your government did that today?

So Joseph confiscated all of the grain and all of the money from the people of Egypt and Canaan, but still, famine gripped the land. We don't know for sure, but it seems plausible that Joseph continued to collect any new monies the people came to possess—talk about zero "cash flow!"

We can also assume that the price of grain, as one would expect in a severe famine, was ridiculously high. Now, I don't think these people had much in the way of emergency cash on hand for difficult times before the famine struck, but we know they had absolutely none after Joseph put the second phase of his plan into effect.

"When the money of the people of Egypt and Canaan was gone, all Egypt came to Joseph and said, 'Give us food. Why should we die before your eyes? Our money is all gone.'" [1]

We do not, of course, have economic statistics for ancient Egypt, but as I said, it's likely that high demand and low supply caused the price of food to skyrocket. By the way, that's exactly what you could expect today with any interruption in the food supply. Consider how much food is in your house. Then think about how much food is on hand at your local grocery store. How long would it all last if the trucks couldn't deliver more? My guess is—not long. So the loss of money—liquid resources—needed to buy the little amount of food available was the first problem experienced by the people of Egypt and Canaan. But that was only the beginning.

---

[1] Genesis 47:15

In order to survive the severe long-term famine they were experiencing, the people next had to part with their non-cash assets.

"'Then bring your livestock,' said Joseph. 'I will sell you food in exchange for your livestock, since your money is gone.' So they brought their livestock to Joseph, and he gave them food in exchange for their horses, their sheep and goats, their cattle and donkeys. And he brought them through that year with food in exchange for all their livestock." [2]

What would you do if your money ran out and you had no way to make more? Few of us today have livestock to sell, so what would you sell to buy food? You'd probably part with a fishing boat, a second car, and even your house if it came to it. In Joseph's day, non-cash assets meant livestock, and selling that was far more painful than parting with an RV today. Livestock requires care and feeding, but it's also a potential source of income from the sale of milk, wool and offspring. *Parting with it hurt badly.*

Then consider that when the people of Egypt sold their livestock, the value of anything that required feeding and upkeep (without grain) was probably at its lowest. So while this non-cash asset normally was worth a lot, in a time of famine, it likely had little value. A good comparison today would be large fuel-demanding vehicles in times of high gasoline prices. Recently, a man told me he donated his older model SUV just to get a tax break because he couldn't find a buyer at any price!

So Joseph confiscated the people's grain, money and livestock, but the famine continued. What, if anything, did the people have left to offer Joseph in exchange for their survival?

"'Buy us and our land in exchange for food, and we with our land will be in bondage to Pharaoh. Give us seed so that we may live and not die, and that the land may not become desolate.'" [3]

[2] Genesis 47:16-17
[3] Genesis 47:19

Can you imagine selling yourself to the government in exchange for your life? If that seems far-fetched, consider that once the government takes away your income, savings, food and other non-cash assets, aren't you a slave already?

"So Joseph bought all the land in Egypt for Pharaoh. The Egyptians, one and all, sold their fields, because the famine was too severe for them. The land became Pharaoh's, and Joseph reduced the people to servitude, from one end of Egypt to the other." [4]

For the people of ancient Egypt, selling their land was an act of utter capitulation. They had abandoned all hope, so really, throwing themselves into the bargain probably meant little to them. This final act was one of pure desperation for the people of Egypt. As in any agrarian economy, land was the basis of their wealth and their personal sustainability. To have any hope of rebuilding their assets, they had to have land to plant grain and forage. Without it, they couldn't keep livestock.

So the people had become slaves of the Pharaoh, an entire nation in abject servitude to its government. We've seen the brutal actions of totalitarian dictators in modern times—Mao, Stalin, Hitler and Pol Pot top the list. Joseph held even more power over the people of his day than these. We see in his actions, however, the true character of a man after God's heart.

"Joseph said to the people, 'Now that I have bought you and your land today for Pharaoh, here is seed for you so you can plant the ground. But when the crop comes in, give a fifth of it to Pharaoh. The other four-fifths you may keep as seed for the fields and as food for yourselves and your households and your children.'" [5]

A lot of people today would be overjoyed to pay only a 20% flat tax for the use of someone else's resources—in Joseph's case, the land owned by the government. When politicians in free countries make such cavalier statements as, *"You don't ever want a crisis*

---

[4] Genesis 47:20-21
[5] Genesis 47:23-24

to go to waste,"[6] what kind of fair treatment do you think you could get in a dictatorship?

Rather than looking to government in a time of crisis, it's far better to rely on the merciful God who gave you skills and resources to provide for yourself.

The people of ancient Egypt had left themselves no such choice, however. In desperation, the last thing they had to sell was themselves—their freedom. The famine had taken everything and they had no other way to survive. This is an epic picture of being unprepared for a disaster of biblical proportions.

I'm from the Pharoah and I'm Here to Help

A key lesson from this first major famine is that the *government* did the saving, not the people. It was a government savings program, radically contrary to how the Bible tells us to prepare for difficult times—which is as individuals. Joseph was used by God to lead the government to prepare, because the people, it appears, did not prepare for their own survival. I would never presume that God will always provide a Joseph during times of crisis. God's will is that we prepare for times of trouble ourselves.

A second lesson is that the government did not give the grain back to the people. It sold the food back them. This is a significant point. Joseph's plan was not a welfare program. The government, even under Joseph's benevolent direction, still took everything the people had in the midst of their suffering. Imagine what horrors await an unprepared people at the hands of a less compassionate leader.

Too many of us assume that if the government has all the resources and we're all hungry, the government will take care of us.

---

[6] Rahm Emanuel, former Chief of Staff in the Obama White House (now Mayor of Chicago) quoted in "Obama, Assembling Team, Turns to the Economy," *The New York Times*, November 7, 2008. (http://www.nytimes.com/2008/11/07/us/politics/07obama. html?pagewanted=print)

I would suggest that the degree to which a government remains responsive to the needs of the people is in reverse proportion to the amount of power it holds. Totalitarian governments have notoriously little compassion. If you don't believe me, ask the people of North Korea, where food is always in critically short supply. At least in Egypt there was grain for Joseph to sell back to the people.

There's yet a third lesson to glean from the story of Joseph and the famine. When he was put in charge, Joseph began a seven-year program of preparation for the anticipated crisis. That's important. It takes time to get prepared. You can't do it overnight. As individuals and families, we need to have a long-term outlook for preparation. I don't even think seven years is too long. I wouldn't advise waiting seven years to get started, however. In the coming chapters, I'll tell you how to get started now with what I call The S.A.L.T. Plan™, but more on that later.

As we begin to think about preparing for difficult times, it's important to remember that God never causes disasters to strike His people, but He does use them to discipline us, to shape our character, to draw us closer to Him, and sometimes, to demonstrate certain principles. In the case of Joseph and the first great famine, I believe God showed His wisdom in the manner through which He saved and preserved His people. It was a lesson that we must turn to Him for guidance in the midst of economic calamity. We must do what He has revealed will preserve us, not what the world would have us do.

There is nothing in the story of the first great famine about man's wisdom. The Pharaoh's dream came from God. Joseph was sent by God to that place at that time to carry out His will. It is a story about God's wisdom expressed through Joseph to save 20% of the nation's grain for seven years that ultimately saved His people.

We learn from this famine that we must be people, like Joseph, who save for the days of economic famine and are therefore in a position to save God's people.

CHAPTER
FOUR

ELIJAH AND THE SECOND GREAT FAMINE

Big Brother or Big Idol?

I n *The Root of Riches*, I wrote that a name we seldom, if ever, use for God is "Jealous." Yet Scripture warns that it is, in fact, one of the names we can use to address the Lord:

"Do not worship any other god, for the Lord, whose name is Jealous, is a jealous God." [1]

In humans, jealousy is usually a character flaw, but for God, the only One who is worthy of worship, jealousy is a thoroughly righteous response when His people begin to worship anything but Him. He has made this abundantly clear, with no "wiggle room" whatsoever, in the very first of the Ten Commandments:

"I am the Lord your God, who brought you out of Egypt, out of the land of slavery. You shall have no other gods before me." [2]

Most believers would readily accept that worshiping—making a false idol—of money or material possessions is a big problem. Some even recognize that reserving too much of our affection for our favorite sports team or a cherished hobby is not a good thing. But how many of us completely ignore our growing dependence on *government* to solve our problems and provide for our needs? What percentage of citizens in the western nations today think that government is more important economically than God? It wouldn't surprise me if it were half of the population.

Our leaders know this perfectly well, and I daresay most of them believe it as well. When public policy is geared toward making people more dependent on government than on God, do you think He turns a blind eye? Do you think He is incapable of making a government accountable to Him?

As we look across the landscape of the West today, we see coun-

---

[1] Genesis 34:14
[2] Exodus 20:2-3

try after country on the verge of economic collapse—self-made "victims" of their own foolish policies. They have rejected God and His financial principles, replacing Him with inventions of their own.

For 150 years, U.S. currency has carried the motto, "In God We Trust." Put yourself in His shoes for just a minute, and imagine the righteous anger He must feel when He sees a government involved in trusting anything but Him.

God doesn't have to send locusts to make His disapproval known; He can simply withhold His blessing. Are we beginning to see signs of divine disapproval now, as nations teeter on the brink of bankruptcy?

Next we'll look at what happens when a government actually makes public policy out of the worship of false idols.

Ahab—Just about the Worst King Ever

First Kings 18 records the events of the second great biblical famine, this one lasting only about half as long as the seven year epic event in Egypt. In those times, Ahab was King of Israel and he had a very bad reputation In fact, God's Word says Ahab was the worst king:

"Ahab son of Omri did more evil in the eyes of the Lord than any of those before him. He not only considered it trivial to commit the sins of Jeroboam son of Nebat [idolatry], but he also married Jezebel daughter of Ethbaal king of the Sidonians, and began to serve Baal and worship him. He set up an altar for Baal in the temple of Baal that he built in Samaria. Ahab also made an Asherah pole and did more to arouse the anger of the Lord, the God of Israel, than did all the kings of Israel before him." [3]

---

[3] 1 Kings 16:29-33

None of this, of course, escaped the Lord's notice. So He used economics to get Ahab's attention. God directed the prophet Elijah to declare to Ahab that it would not rain over the next several years, *"...except at my [Elijah's] word."* [4] Talk about being instantly unpopular! Promising a drought in those days was the equivalent of putting a death sentence on your own head. Ahab was already unpopular; a drought-induced famine would likely cause the people of Israel to rebel against him. No wonder God then told Elijah to move out of town and hide in a ravine. Making kings angry is dangerous business.

The Trouble Begins

Meanwhile, as you would expect, God was true to His word—it stopped raining in Israel—and we can only assume that without rain, there were no crops. Without crops, there could be no food. In fact, it seems that food became so scarce that God sent ravens carrying meat and bread to Elijah at his hideout in the Kerith Ravine just to keep him alive.

Today, famine is simply not part of the mindset of people in the affluent western nations. The closest we get to famine is hearing news stories about food shortages in Ethiopia or Somalia. The U.S. has never known a famine of any significant size or duration, and even our poor can be overweight.

In fact, food is so abundant and cheap in the West that we take its continued supply completely for granted. School children are often surprised to learn that eggs come from chickens, not grocery stores!

The truth is, our affluence and the resulting lack of knowledge about what it takes to produce food makes us more *vulnerable*, not less, to the painful consequences of an interruption in the food

[4] 1 Kings 17:1

supply. Most people in the West have no idea how to grow the food they would need to survive if an economic collapse causes an interruption in the food supply. Eighty years ago, during the Great Depression, far more people had gardens and put food aside than today. We've all seen pictures of the long soup lines that formed back then when people had no food. Just imagine how long those lines would be today.

It was drought, not an economic collapse, that caused famine in Elijah's day. It hadn't rained for nearly three years. Food was scarce, and probably quite expensive. We can assume that the people had by then gone through the first phase of a famine (or economic collapse), the loss of their money. Remember, at such a time, income is hard to come by and food is expensive. With their money gone, their non-cash assets, livestock, were threatened next. Even the unrighteous King Ahab knew that things were beginning to get desperate:

"Now the famine was severe in Samaria, and Ahab had summoned Obadiah, his palace administrator....Ahab had said to Obadiah, 'Go through the land to all the springs and valleys. Maybe we can find some grass to keep the horses and mules alive so we will not have to kill any of our animals.'" [5]

Ahab sent Obadiah out to find more than grass. The entire economy of Israel was probably on the verge of collapse. Ahab needed to find Elijah and get him to make it rain as God had directed— and fast. So he sent Obadiah and everyone else to find the old prophet. Obadiah says as much to Elijah when he stumbled upon the man of God while searching for grass:

"As surely as the Lord your God lives, there is not a nation or kingdom where my master has not sent someone to look for you." [6]

God had gotten Ahab's undivided attention. The kingdom was in danger of losing all of its assets. God had used famine to

---

[5] 1 Kings 18:2-3, 5

bring the nation of Israel to its senses and to look to God for its economic deliverance. Ahab and his wife Jezebel were feeding the prophets of Baal at their table. So the government had not only endorsed idolatry, but by Ahab feeding the prophets of Baal, he was giving the people's money to support it. Not surprisingly, God had had enough. The stage was set for an epic showdown, and that would happen soon at Mount Carmel.

All the best showdowns begin with a challenge, and that's exactly what Elijah did—he called out Ahab. Elijah came out of hiding and presented himself to the deviant and dangerous king. That must have taken courage!

I think it's fascinating that just like some politicians today, when confronted on his policies, Ahab tried to shift the blame for his kingdom's problems onto someone else—in this case, Elijah!

"Is that you, you troubler of Israel?" [7]

Now, Elijah, who wasn't about to accept that untrue criticism, fired back at Ahab—

"I have not made trouble for Israel…But you and your father's family have. You have abandoned the Lord's commands and have followed the Baals. Now summon the people from all over Israel to meet me on Mount Carmel. And bring the four hundred and fifty prophets of Baal and the four hundred prophets of Asherah, who eat at Jezebel's table." [8]

Do you see what's happening here? This is shaping up just like an old western movie with a dual in full public view. Elijah had publicly challenged Ahab to a duel, and Ahab couldn't back down without looking like a coward.

[6] 1 Kings 18:10

"Fire Fight" on Mount Carmel

"So Ahab sent word throughout all Israel and assembled the prophets on Mount Carmel. Elijah went before the people and said, 'How long will you waver between two opinions? If the Lord is God, follow him; but if Baal is God, follow him.' But the people said nothing." [9]

Can't you just see the people of Israel looking confused and unsure about which side they should back? Elijah knew he would have to demonstrate exactly whose God was in control!

"Then Elijah said to them, 'I am the only one of the Lord's prophets left, but Baal has four hundred and fifty prophets. Get two bulls for us. Let Baal's prophets choose one for themselves, and let them cut it into pieces and put it on the wood but not set fire to it. I will prepare the other bull and put it on the wood but not set fire to it. Then you call on the name of your god, and I will call on the name of the Lord. The god who answers by fire—he is God.'" [10]

That seemed like a "win-win" for the hesitant people of Israel, who immediately agreed to the "contest."

"Elijah said to the prophets of Baal, 'Choose one of the bulls and prepare it first, since there are so many of you. Call on the name of your god, but do not light the fire.' So they took the bull given them and prepared it. Then they called on the name of Baal from morning till noon. 'Baal, answer us!' they shouted. But there was no response; no one answered. And they danced around the altar they had made." [11]

Imagine how Elijah must have enjoyed the spectacle of a bunch of fools dancing around an altar to a god that didn't exist! After a few hours, Elijah increased the intensity of the challenge.

---

[7] 1 Kings 18:17   [8] 1 Kings 18:18-19   [9] 1 Kings 18:20-21   [10] 1 Kings 18:25-26
[11] 1 Kings 18:27-29

"At noon Elijah began to taunt them. 'Shout louder!' he said. '
Surely he is a god! Perhaps he is deep in thought, or busy, or travel-
ing. Maybe he is sleeping and must be awakened.' So they shouted
louder and slashed themselves with swords and spears, as was their
custom, until their blood flowed. Midday passed, and they continued
their frantic prophesying until the time for the evening sacrifice. But
there was no response, no one answered, no one paid attention." [12]

Well, they'd had their chance, so Elijah gathered the people
around and prepared another altar for the Lord's sacrifice. He
placed wood on the altar, cut another bull into pieces and had it
arranged on top, and then (I think this is a nice touch!) had the
altar drenched with water three times.

"At the time of sacrifice, the prophet Elijah stepped forward and
prayed: 'Lord, the God of Abraham, Isaac and Israel, let it be known
today that you are God in Israel and that I am your servant and
have done all these things at your command. Answer me, Lord, an-
swer me, so these people will know that you, Lord, are God, and that
you are turning their hearts back again.'" [13]

Safe to say, the Lord did not disappoint:

"Then the fire of the Lord fell and burned up the sacrifice, the
wood, the stones and the soil...." [14]

Can you imagine the dread in the hearts of the prophets of Baal?
They must have guessed that they were "toast" too. Meanwhile,
the Lord's pyrotechnic display had an immediate and profound
effect on the wayward children of Israel:

"When all the people saw this, they fell prostrate and cried,
'The Lord—he is God! The Lord—he is God!'

[12] 1 Kings 18:27-29
[13] 1 Kings 18:36-37
[14] 1 Kings 18:38

*"Then Elijah commanded them, 'Seize the prophets of Baal.
Don't let anyone get away!' They seized them, and Elijah had them
brought down to the Kishon Valley and slaughtered there."* [15]

Of course, you know that after the people humbled themselves before the Lord, the rains returned. Crops grew again and the famine was lifted.

It's interesting to note that the people killed the prophets of Baal, but they did not overthrow Ahab. The errant king eventually repented and was allowed to die in battle some time later. His wife Jezebel, however, was not nearly as fortunate. She had strongly influenced Ahab to worship Baal, and was condemned to be eaten by dogs.

This is a picture of God purging a government of idolatry and corruption. Is there any reason to believe He wouldn't do the same today?

The lesson from this famine is to serve God, not the gods of the culture. Idolatry remains an affront to the Lord, our Provider. His name remains Jealous. Notice too that although Elijah had to flee to survive the three and a half year famine, God supernaturally provided for his needs.

[15] 1 Kings 18:39-40

CHAPTER FIVE

ELISHA AND THE THIRD GREAT FAMINE

At Least There Wasn't a Plague

The third major biblical famine I want us to examine is recorded in 2 Kings 6-7, during the time of Elisha, the protégé of Elijah. Scripture tells us that the price of food skyrocketed, as it always does with high demand and low supply. This famine may well have been the worst so far because, unlike the others, it was accompanied by war.

The nation of Israel had been divided into two separate kingdoms after the death of Solomon in 931 BC: Israel and Judah. The House of David ruled the Kingdom of Judah in the south from its capital at Jerusalem. The Kingdom of Israel, just to the north, had its own capital behind protective walls at a place called Samaria. It was there that war—and famine—struck.

Despite a peace treaty ratified earlier between the kingdoms of Syria and Israel, the nations continued to make war against each other. In 2 Kings 6:24, we see that the king of Syria has gathered up all of his troops and invaded Israel, the northern Jewish kingdom.

The invading force must have been substantial, because the Syrians were able to completely surround the entire capital city of Samaria, laying siege to it. We know that the Syrians prevented food from coming into the city. That is, of course, the whole point of a siege—to starve your enemy into coming out and surrendering. We don't know how much time elapsed before the siege was eventually lifted by God's miraculous intervention. It seems likely, however, that the siege produced famine much more quickly than drought or a similar drawn out crop failure. With no food coming into the city at all, it didn't take long for things to get desperate.

What's a Shekel Worth These Days?

In the case of the siege of Samaria, we can get a clear idea of the economic impact of famine. Scripture actually names commodities and prices.

"There was a great famine in the city; the siege lasted so long that a donkey's head sold for eighty shekels of silver, and a quarter of a cab of seed pods for five shekels." [1]

Now, I don't know about you, but donkey head is not on my list of favorite foods. Further, it was not only unappetizing, but just as unclean as swine to the people of ancient Israel. The donkey is, however, a highly useful work animal, so we can determine that the people trapped inside the city of Samaria had entered the second phase of famine, selling (and eating) their livestock. And with so little food available, the value of money was near worthless. After all, you can't eat it. That a donkey's head was selling for two pounds[2] of silver shows how desperate things had become. The famine had caused hyper-inflation, at least with the price of anything that could be eaten. Not even the king could escape the cries of the people.

"As the king of Israel was passing by on the wall, a woman cried to him, 'Help me, my lord the king!' The king replied, 'If the Lord does not help you, where can I get help for you? From the threshing floor? From the winepress?'" [3]

The King, in a moment of humility, recognized that only God had the power to end his people's suffering. He may not have been happy about it, but at least he recognized his own limitations.

[1] 2 Kings 6:25

[2] New Geneva Study Bible, Foundation for Reformation, 1995. See study note at 2 Kings 6:25, pg. 525.

[3] 2 Kings 6:26-27

It would seem he had little choice. The war made this famine even more acute and painful than the others. Obviously, it brought death and destruction, as do all wars. But as earlier noted, the siege immediately cut off all food from getting into the city. Also, it seems to have eliminated any possibility of a "third phase" of famine—selling yourself into slavery just to stay alive. Apparently this was a fight to the death; the Syrians would take no prisoners, which was not the custom in those days.[4] At least the people of Samaria must have believed they had no other option; only that could explain sinking to the level of depravity described by the woman in her conversation with the king:

"Then he asked her, 'What's the matter?'

"She answered, 'This woman said to me, "Give up your son so we may eat him today, and tomorrow we'll eat my son." So we cooked my son and ate him. The next day I said to her, 'Give up your son so we may eat him,' but she had hidden him.'" [5]

We don't know with certainty the identity of this unnamed king, but many scholars believe it was Jehoram (Joram), the son of Ahab.[6] In any case, his reaction to the crisis of famine in his land was exactly the same as Ahab's—blame the Lord's prophet—in this case, Elisha.

"When the king heard the woman's words, he tore his robes. As he went along the wall, the people looked, and they saw that, under his robes, he had sackcloth on his body. He said, 'May God deal with me, be it ever so severely, if the head of Elisha son of Shaphat remains on his shoulders today!'" [7]

---

[4] See Deuteronomy 20:10-11
[5] 2 Kings 6:28-29
[6] See 2 Kings 3:1-3
[7] 2 Kings 6:30-31

God's Sovereignty over the Economy

In this third great famine, we see God's hand at work right down to the prices of individual, named commodities. This is a tangible demonstration of God's sovereign power over an economy—a power I believe He still exercises today in every nation. If you doubt that He controls every component of every financial system, this story should convince you otherwise.

So the king sent a messenger ahead to find Elisha, but he couldn't wait to hear word of the prophet's whereabouts. Instead, the king set out after his own messenger. They arrived at Elisha's house at nearly the same time, to find the city elders meeting with the man of God. Think how that must have irked the king, to find that the movers and shakers of the city were talking with Elisha and not him! At that point, it's easy to envision a red-faced, angry king threatening God's prophet before the assembled elders:

"The King said, 'This disaster is from the Lord. Why should I wait for the Lord any longer?'" [8]

I translate that roughly as, *"This is the Lord's fault. He's not stopping it. You're as close as I can get to Him, so I think I'll lop off your head!"*

Fortunately for the prophet, God gave him exactly the right words to say. Now, remember that just then, a donkey's head was selling for at least two pounds of silver. Some writers put the value at five to eight pounds of silver. It's impossible to say, for sure, but undoubtedly the price of donkey heads and anything else that could be eaten had reached astronomical levels. But the Lord was about to step in.

"Elisha replied, 'Hear the word of the Lord. This is what the

---

[8] 2 Kings 6:33

*Lord says: About this time tomorrow, a seah of the finest flour will
sell for a shekel and two seahs of barley for a shekel at the gate of
Samaria.'"*[9]

Now, to the group assembled in Elisha's living room that must
have sounded completely insane. The Syrian army surrounded the
entire city. No food had been allowed in for perhaps two years.
People were eating their own children! Here Elisha is saying that
in 24 hours, the equivalent of seven quarts of premium flour will
cost less than a half-ounce of silver.[10] It was so absurd that the
king's officer doubted that even God could pull that off. I know—
you have to wonder how they could have become so skeptical and
jaded—but that's how bad things had gotten in the city.

*"The officer on whose arm the king was leaning said to the
man of God, 'Look, even if the Lord should open the floodgates of the
heavens, could this happen?'"*

That "officer" of the king was not necessarily a military man. I
like to think that he was an economist who advised the king on
the price of commodities, but this is only an opinion. My point
is that economists or "advisors" can certainly be wrong, and it's
never a good idea to doubt the power of the Lord to intervene in
economic matters, as we shall see.

It's interesting to note that the only other place in Scripture where
we find the term "floodgates of heaven" is the famous Malachi
3:10, which is also the only place in Scripture where the Lord
invites us to test Him. So here we have the king's advisors telling
him, *"Yeah, sure! This guy is wrong. He's foolish. This cannot happen.
Even if God opens the floodgates of heaven, prices are not going to fall
that much by tomorrow morning."*

Elisha not only stood firm, he also confronted the unbelief of the
rational skeptic:

[9] 2 Kings 7:1
[10] New Geneva Study Bible, pg. 526. See note at 2 Kings 7:1.

"'You will see it with your own eyes,' answered Elisha, 'but you will not eat any of it!'" [11]

Well, certainly it would take a miracle for the price of food to drop that fast overnight, and of course, that's precisely what happened.

Outside the gates of the city, in the darkness of night, the Lord caused the Syrian army to "hear footsteps"—the sounds of a huge advancing mercenary force they thought had been hired by the king of Israel to destroy them. Of course, there was no such force, but the Syrians panicked, and to a man fled back to their homeland, leaving behind all of their food, weapons, horses, donkeys (heads and all), clothing, silver and gold. Not only was the siege lifted immediately, but the vast stores of food and supplies abandoned by the Syrians were immediately taken into the city, causing the price of flour and other food items to plummet.

"Then the people went out and plundered the tents of the Syrians. So a seah of fine flour was sold for a shekel, and two seahs of barley for a shekel, according to the word of the Lord." [12]

Unlike economists and stockbrokers today, Elisha, at the Lord's direction, was able to predict the *commodity*, the *quantity*, the *price*, and the *time* and *location* that the price would change, right down to the shekel. He could have made a fortune in the futures market!

Oh, and remember the king's officer, the man who doubted God's ability to control the price of food? Elisha had promised the man that he'd see those prices drop with his own eyes, but that he wouldn't taste any of it. Well, as it happened, that same officer was on hand the next day when the starving masses rushed to get the food as it was brought through the gate.

[11] 2 Kings 7:2
[12] 2 Kings 7:16 (NKJV)

"And that is exactly what happened to him, for the people trampled him in the gateway, and he died." [13]

What a picture of God's dramatic and unpredictable deliverance of His people. What a shocking and sudden demise of the king's advisor who doubted God's power over the economy.

There is one overriding lesson to be gleaned from the story of the third great famine—that God is perfectly capable of controlling an economy—right down to the price of a cup of grain and that should bring us to the end of any attitude of self-reliance. We are to be God-reliant in good times and bad.

[13] 2 Kings 7:20

CHAPTER
SIX

AGABUS AND THE FOURTH
GREAT FAMINE

Agabus and the Fourth Great Famine

The first century church in Jerusalem was marked by severe persecution from both the Romans and the Pharisees. Paradoxically, it was also a time marked by a viral spread of Christianity as well as complete terror among early believers. To be outspoken about the Gospel could cause a spontaneous riot. Believers were often taken by mobs demanding their imprisonment or worse—stoning was not uncommon.

These new believers, all Jews, found themselves struggling for their existence as well as the very survival of the infant church. This persecution caused them to grow closer to Christ and each other as they stood up to this severe test of their faith.

In Acts 4, they are described as being "one in heart and mind." Remarkably, their mission was of such great importance to them that they abandoned their personal agendas and claims to their possessions.

"No one claimed that any of his possessions was his own, but they shared everything they had." [1]

This unity and willingness to sacrifice marked the transformation taking place in what was otherwise a materialistic, hedonistic culture. It was evidence of the reality of the resurrection of Christ.

The fledgling church needed believers helping and supporting each other to grow. But how was that accomplished? As it turned out, the church survived and grew with the resources already in the possession of the converts.

"There were no needy persons among them. For from time to time those who owned land or houses sold them, brought the money from the sales and put it at the apostles' feet, and it was distributed to anyone as he had need." [2]

[1] Acts 4:32
[2] Acts 4:34-35

As I write these words, the United States and several European countries are witnessing public protests by the "Occupy" movement. It is ostensibly an outcry against the greed of the rich, defined as the 1%. The protestors' expressed agenda is to bring about financial "fairness" by taxing the rich.

The government is incapable of legislating away greed. Greed is a condition of the human heart and is only eradicated by a change of beliefs and a shift in values. What these protestors may not realize is that they are calling for the wrong god to solve the problem of greed. God, not government is the only one able to transform the hearts of people.

Much to my shock, many of these "Occupy" protestors are professing to be Christians. They believe that since the Church is not helping the poor (or them), government should cause a redistribution of wealth through taxes.

As we look at those remarkable expressions of generosity in the early church, we see no hint of a government program causing an outpouring of love and generosity. It was driven by an individual choice and an overwhelming desire to accomplish God's purposes. It is a beautiful picture of the role of the early Church and a funding model that continues to this day.

You must understand two important points before we take a close look at the fourth great biblical famine.

First, the early church was supported by the sale of assets—land and homes. Notice they were not making small contributions out of their cash flow. This passage does not say that they began tithing or giving $25 a month, but that those who were able sold their assets and turned the proceeds over to the control and trust of the elders.

This is important to remember. The day may come, during some economic crisis, when the Church must again be funded in this way. God may call upon us to liquidate our assets to support His work. We must be prepared to put a greater value on the Kingdom than a business, home, land, jewelry, gold or a 401(k). As did the early believers, we must be ready to demonstrate our priorities with a tangible expression of love for one another.

Second, this passage goes on to describe how a particular Levite from Cyprus named Joseph liquidated assets for the church. We learn that the apostles had an affectionate name for this brother—Barnabas—by which we know him today. Barnabas means "Son of Encouragement." Obviously, his generosity made him a welcome and endeared member of the newly formed "family." Perhaps one day you too will be called upon to be a Son or Daughter of Encouragement during an economic crisis.

Barnabas not only invested his money in the Church, he gave his entire life, traveling far and wide to offer support and wise counsel. Barnabas was likely among the first to be called "Christian."

"Now those who had been scattered by the persecution in connection with Stephen traveled as far as Phoenicia, Cyprus and Antioch, telling the message only to Jews. Some of them, however, men from Cyprus and Cyrene, went to Antioch and began to speak to Greeks also, telling them the good news about the Lord Jesus. The Lord's hand was with them, and a great number of people believed and turned to the Lord.

"News of this reached the ears of the church at Jerusalem, and they sent Barnabas to Antioch. When he arrived and saw the evidence of the grace of God, he was glad and encouraged them all to remain true to the Lord with all their hearts. He was a good man, full of the Holy Spirit and faith, and a great number of people were brought to the Lord.

"Then Barnabas went to Tarsus to look for Saul, and when he found him, he brought him to Antioch. So for a whole year Barnabas and Saul met with the church and taught great numbers of people. The disciples were called Christians first at Antioch." [3]

As the Church continued to grow, the need to identify the converts as a distinct group must have become clear. There would be no reason to call them something different if it appeared the movement would soon pass away and everyone would go back to their former identities. But these were no longer Jews, Samaritans or Gentiles—they were a people different and unique. They were Christians. The Church was here to stay.

It must have been a time of great joy and celebration as many were brought to the Lord and unified in Christ. Soon, however, the faith of the new believers would be put to an extreme test—famine was coming again to God's people.

"During this time some prophets came down from Jerusalem to Antioch. One of them, named Agabus, stood up and through the Spirit predicted that a severe famine would spread over the entire Roman world. (This happened during the reign of Claudius.)" [4]

The church in its fragile early years not only survived severe persecution, but also grew and spread as a result of the scattering of the saints to regions beyond Jerusalem. Soon the disciples even began adding Greeks to the family of Christians. Those must have been heady times in the outpost called Antioch—until Agabus cut the celebrations short with his prophecy of famine for not only Israel, but the "entire Roman world." This would literally be an economic event of "biblical proportions."

The disciples must have been shocked and disappointed. Who could blame them for perhaps thinking, *What on earth is God up to now? This is the last thing that we need! First we are persecuted, now we're going to starve?*

[3] Acts 11:19-26
[4] Acts 11:27-28

But remember, these are many of the same people who experienced that deep transformation of the heart back in Jerusalem—the same people who were so unified in purpose as to turn over all of their possessions to the Church. Now this unity would be severely tested. Would they quit and run? Would they stop giving? Would they stockpile and hoard? Would they abandon the mission and become survivalists?

A better question might be, "Do we have the same degree of faith exhibited by these early believers?" As we shall see, they set the bar very high, indeed.

"The disciples, each according to his ability, decided to provide help for the brothers living in Judea. This they did, sending their gift to the elders by Barnabas and Saul." [5]

Those disciples at Antioch, true followers of Christ, seized the opportunity to share what little they had. It is an amazing response in the moment of truth. Led by the example of Barnabas, "a good man, full of the Holy Spirit and faith," they demonstrated the same maturity.

Remember that Barnabas had earlier "encouraged them to remain true to the Lord with all their hearts." This meant more than a casual commitment; it was a total sense of duty to be faithful to God's cause. It led these new believers, many of them Gentiles, to share with others who were suffering as a result of the famine. It should be noted that while Scripture reveals Jews practiced charity toward others, this virtue was largely unknown throughout the Roman Empire until the rise of Christianity.[6]

This verse seems so consistent with what we would expect of believers at the time that we almost miss its impact. In a culture of greed, selfishness, indulgence, luxury and "every man for himself," the world must have expected those believers to abandon

---

[5] Acts 11:29-30

this strange sect—to acknowledge that the cost of following Jesus was just too high. The world was wrong.

Not only did they not abandon their faith, they refused to follow the natural human desire to hoard—these new Christians instead shared their resources during a time of suffering.

What an incredible witness this must have been to those who observed the giving and to those who received that support. I have a mental of picture of the Enemy watching from afar and shaking his ugly head in disbelief. *"They did it again. They passed another test. This Church is going to be more difficult to stop than I thought."*

I believe Barnabas and Saul and all the believers in the early church were prepared in their hearts and minds for the persecution, the famine, the trials and the testing. They were His hands and feet ready to meet the needs of others when the world least expected it. They knew they were called to be salt, the preservative of the beautiful and matchless Gospel of Jesus Christ, and today, we have the same opportunity.

[6] Schmidt, Alvin J., *Under the Influence: How Christianity Transformed Civilization,* Zondervan Publishing House, 2001, pp. 130-131.

The S.A.L.T. Plan

CHAPTER
SEVEN

THE FAILURE OF
SELF-RELIANCE

A Curse Fulfilled?

Among the many lessons of the great biblical famines there is one moral that requires special treatment—the failure of self-reliance.

This is not an argument for government-enforced collectivism in any form, which is a failed idea of Man that inspires the most vicious examples of selfishness. The story of Joseph and his benevolent survival program is the exception to the horrors of involuntary collectivism, which always requires violence or the threat of violence to force compliance. We should not forget that Joseph was a deeply faithful man after God's heart—a rare trait among dictators.

Greed and fear are powerful forces in the human mind. Only through a transformation of the heart are we freed from them—the kind of change that takes place when we accept Christ as Lord and Savior and follow His humble example:

"When he had finished washing their feet, he put on his clothes and returned to his place. 'Do you understand what I have done for you?' he asked them. 'You call me "Teacher"and "Lord," and rightly so, for that is what I am. Now that I, your Lord and Teacher, have washed your feet, you also should wash one another's feet. I have set you an example that you should do as I have done for you. I tell you the truth, no servant is greater than his master, nor is a messenger greater than the one who sent him. Now that you know these things, you will be blessed if you do them.'" [1]

To be sure, Jesus wanted His disciples to care for and nurture each other, to sacrifice themselves for the good of others, as He did. But we see a little further in this passage that Jesus had a deeper reason for this action than simple survival:

---

[1] John 13:12-17

"A new command I give you: Love one another. As I have loved you, so you must love one another. By this all men will know that you are my disciples, if you love one another." [2]

One reason the early Church spread so rapidly was that Christ's disciples obeyed His commandment and put others before self. This willingness to show love and generosity caused these Christ followers to stand in bold contrast to a culture marked by greed and self-reliance. This, in turn, drew others in to hear the saving message of the Gospel, and so it spread.

Nowhere is this more evident than in the story of the fourth great famine, where Gentile believers gave their resources to save others, predominantly Jews, whom they had likely never laid eyes upon.

This example of generosity, when the giver's personal needs are great, stands in stark contrast to events in the earlier famines, particularly the third, in which the capital city of Israel was laid siege.

While some were on the brink of starvation, others engaged in profiteering inside the walls of Samaria, demanding bars of silver for a donkey head. Don't misunderstand—I'm all for the free market fluctuation of prices. Whenever the government steps in to control the price of a commodity, it only makes matters worse. But in this case, money had little practical value. You can't eat it.

Still, it seems people refused to share what little they had with their starving neighbors. It was every man for himself and the sinfulness and greed of Mankind was on full display. These horrible events seem to fulfill one of the many curses God warned would befall a rebellious people.

"Therefore in your midst parents will eat their children, and children will eat their parents. I will inflict punishment on you and will scatter all your survivors to the winds." [3]

[2] John 13:34-35
[3] Ezekiel 5:10

The scattering would come later when Samaria and the northern kingdom fell to another invasion. The point here, however, is that when things get really bad, when the wheels start to come off an economy, as God's people we are to band together and take care of each other, but we see anything but that in the third great famine.

In the days ahead, some will hoard and keep all they can for themselves. Others will gouge their suffering brothers and sisters. But Christians should be prepared to seize every opportunity to share what they have with their neighbors who may have nothing. And that's precisely why I think God's people need to prepare now to be salt and light in a darkening world.

Facing the Scoffers

It takes great faith to share with your neighbors when food is scarce, when you're not sure if you have enough for your own family. You can't do it without believing deep in your heart that God is your True Provider and the Owner of everything.

The incident with Elisha and the king's officer is a great example. Elisha had overwhelming faith that the Lord would step in to end the famine—that He would save His people. The officer's reaction to Elisha's prediction of food prices dropping embodies the belief of self-reliance. *"We're on our own. God can't save us, even if He opens the floodgates of heaven."*

That sort of tension—between the man who trusts God and the scoffer—exists today all around us. It's the tension between the world's view of the economy and the spiritual view; Man's economy versus God's economy. Our role, as believers, is to bring a spiritual view to a world still clinging to the failure of Man's ways. Are you prepared to face the scoffers of our day?

The self-reliance or "survival" industry is growing in America. The Internet is loaded with ads urging people to buy emergency food caches, gold, guns and other survival gear. Several companies are selling non-hybridized seeds that produce fertile offspring to ensure future crops—just in case seeds become unavailable. Maybe that's a good idea, but one thing's for certain—none of those ads are pitching the idea of sharing with your neighbors. It's all about self-reliance, self-survival—self, self, self! *"We're on our own, because God can't save us."*

That mindset is evident in most political leaders today, as well, although expressed somewhat differently. *"We have to fix the economy, because God can't do it. Maybe if we tweak it a little more, borrow a little more, spend a little more, tax a little more, the economy will recover and we can all keep our jobs."*

Never mind that God's financial principles work every time and everywhere they're tried—with individuals, businesses, and nations. Work hard and be productive, live within your means, save and be generous with others. Understand that God owns everything, and you are merely His steward. Do these things and He will pour His blessings upon you. These principles made the United States the wealthiest and most powerful nation in history. But we stand today on a precipice.

What happens then, when we take God out of the public square? What are the consequences of removing His wisdom from our economic policies? Look around. Personal debt is at an all-time high. Public debt is skyrocketing out of control. Governments are in danger of defaulting on their obligations. Economies are on the verge of collapse. If only our leaders would "get it," but few are ready to admit that Man's ways, once again, have failed.

Sadly, even many Christians doubt that God controls something so small as a nation's economy. We need only look to Scripture and the great famines to see powerful demonstrations of God's ability to deliver His people from destruction—economic and otherwise. God is in control, and we can trust Him in every circumstance of life.

In God We Trust...Really?

Man's economy is filled with false hopes that a "magic bullet" will fix our economic problems. Politicians embrace everything from Keynesian profligate spending to extreme austerity—from a "millionaire's tax" to a national sales tax, to a flat tax or a VAT tax.[4] My prediction is that all of these will be futile if we continue to suffer from spiritual amnesia. Revival must precede any hope of a long-term recovery. We must once again learn to trust God.

The United States once faced an even greater peril than the economic threat it faces today. During the American Civil War, Rev. Mark R. Watkinson, a Baptist minister in Ridleyville, Pennsylvania, was troubled by the fact that U.S. currency at the time carried no recognition of God.

Watkinson wrote to the Secretary of the Treasury, Salmon P. Chase and expressed his concern that if the Union somehow survived, future historians would conclude it was a godless nation. He proposed adding the words "God, Liberty, Law" to U.S. coins.

The pastor's suggestion struck a chord. Secretary Chase immediately ordered the Director of the U.S. Mint at Philadelphia to prepare a new motto for U.S. currency:

"No nation can be strong except in the strength of God, or safe except in His defense. The trust of our people in God should be declared on our national coins.

---

[4] Value Added Tax, used to glean revenue from every stage of production, including the final sale of a product, used mostly in European countries.

"You will cause a device to be prepared without unnecessary delay with a motto expressing in the fewest and tersest words possible this national recognition." [5]

As a result, the humble phrase, *"In God We Trust,"* was added to the nation's coins, and it has remained there for 150 years. The question now for Americans and believers everywhere is, do we still trust in God? Or are we still convinced that Man's ways are the solution?

Those solutions are failing everywhere now, but even if they were to somehow succeed, that return to "prosperity" would be temporary, at best. I see no value in rebuilding or recovering some version of the Golden Calf. We must instead destroy it and once again humble ourselves and accept that there is no hope other than *In God We Trust.*

"For what will it profit a man if he gains the whole world, and loses his own soul?" [6]

[5] "History of 'In God We Trust,'" U.S. Dept. of the Treasury.
[6] Mark 8:36 (NKJV)

PART 3 THREE

THE S.A.L.T. PLAN™

"You are the salt of the earth. But if the salt loses its saltiness, how can it be made salty again? It is no longer good for anything, except to be thrown out and trampled by men."

~ Matthew 5:13

Please note: *The S.A.L.T. Plan*™ is designed to serve you with general guidelines and suggestions. It should not be used in a strict manner. You should employ all available resources you deem necessary for your unique financial situation, including professional financial planning and investment advisors who share your biblical worldview.

CHAPTER
EIGHT

THE S.A.L.T. PLAN DEFINED

If you are to be the salt of the earth, a beacon of light reflecting the glory of your heavenly Father in a darkening world, you need a plan for achieving that end. You need to be intentional now.

This is not a plan to become survivalists, but to be the change agents God purposed for His people. We do this because the one thing every believer should want to hear someday is, *"Well done, good and faithful servant."* [1]

Christians can serve God's purposes during a crisis. Our role is not to build a fortress to hide within but to demonstrate the beauty of believing and practicing God's financial principles that bless others.

To help you prepare, I have developed a simple plan using the acronym S.A.L.T., that stands for:

S = SAVE

A = ASSET ALLOCATION

L = LIQUIDITY

T = TRUTH

[1] Matthew 25:23

Before we look at the individual components of The S.A.L.T. Plan™, we need to lay a firm foundation to build upon. This plan is different from anything you are likely to hear in the months and years ahead.

Basically, there are two messages coming from the world about our looming economic troubles. The first is, "Don't worry, be happy." That is, there's nothing wrong; everything's going to be just fine. While I do believe we should all pray for a financial calamity to be averted, it would be foolish to live as if calamity could not happen.

The second message is, "It's the end of the world, every man for himself!" Actually, there are many examples of nations that experience a financial collapse and recover from it in spite of short-term suffering. The believer who is committed to fulfilling God's will must always reject this self-centered response to danger and be ready to serve others through a crisis.

Here, then, is how The S.A.L.T. Plan™ differs from the messages of the world. Almost everyone has seen those fancy red Swiss Army knives with all the gadgets. Have you ever wondered why you don't see the Swiss army anywhere? You could travel right through Switzerland and never know they had a military force at all. That's because it's a citizen army. Every "soldier" is trained; they keep their personal weapons at home, and they are always prepared to deploy at a moment's notice.

This is the mindset that believers must develop as they prepare for the difficulties ahead. We need to go about our normal routines at work, home and church, but in the background we are always "training," that is, preparing, in case we are called into action.

There is yet another way to view The S.A.L.T. Plan™. We've all seen pictures of vulnerable, low-lying communities destroyed by rising floodwaters. Meteorologists often describe the severity of these events in terms of their likelihood of occurring within a span of time—a 25-year storm, a 50-year storm, and in the most extreme cases—the 100-year storm.

I believe the storm we are facing falls into this latter, severe category, the 100-year storm. That is what we must prepare to face. When photojournalists document the flooding from severe storms, we generally see three types of images. Obviously, there are always individual homes and entire communities damaged or destroyed by rising waters.

Occasionally, we see a home or business surrounded by rising water, but it's safe because the owner managed to pile up sandbags around the structure in the nick of time. We all applaud his effort, and rightfully so.

But consider the herculean effort made to save that structure as flood waters threatened. The owner was entirely consumed with saving his property, and unavailable to help others in need around him. Indeed, perhaps even some of his neighbors helped him pile up sandbags! All things considered, you don't want to be in that position when the storm hits. You want to be ready long before the rain even begins to fall.

The SALT Plan™, then, is not about last-minute sandbags. It's about building a levee around your household that's firmly in place before the trouble starts so that you are prepared not only to weather the storm yourself, but you're also free to help those in need around you.

The photograph on the next page gives you an image of The S.A.L.T. Plan™ in action. The owner may not even be home, but is instead out helping his neighbors. That's the position you want to be in when the rain starts to fall.

The S.A.L.T. Plan™ has four distinct parts. Each is critical to

FLOODWATERS SURROUND FARM HOUSE - FEMA

achieving your goal of preparedness: Saving, Asset Allocation, Liquidity, and Truth.

You are probably thinking, "Saving—no brainer, check. Asset Allocation—how much of what resources to save, okay, makes sense, check. Liquidity—keeping those assets accessible, check. But Truth? What does an intangible like Truth have to do with preparing for a disaster?"

Truth is the cornerstone of the plan because implementing the first three components will avail you nothing if you fail to include Truth. What is that, exactly? For starters, it's humble submission to God's sovereignty and ownership of everything, *including you*. The Truth is that you are only a steward of the resources that God has entrusted to you, nothing more—but equally important—nothing less. As such, you must concern yourself with fulfilling His will, not yours. That alone will make your response to a crisis quite different from that of others around you.

In fact, God's Truth prepares us to serve others regardless of our own needs. Job is a great example of one who suffered loss on every level, yet remained steadfast in His faith and reliance upon God, even when his wife suggested otherwise.

We must rely heavily on God's Word for guidance as we implement The S.A.L.T. Plan™. Without Truth, our efforts might quickly descend into self-reliance and that is definitely not God's will. Our efforts will be radically different from those of the lone survivalist, sitting in his cabin in the mountains, rifle resting on his lap, ready to make his last stand. He's left no room for God in that cabin.

We will dig deeply into the four components of The S.A.L.T. Plan™ in the chapters ahead, giving you the basic framework to begin putting the plan into action. In the process, it is my prayer that you will strengthen your personal finances, your relationships with others and your faith in God that will make you the preservative needed in a financial crisis of biblical proportions.

CHAPTER
NINE

S = SAVINGS

The *Crown Money Map*® Revisited

I f you've seen the *Crown Money Map*®, you know that we have long urged believers to save earnestly. The first savings goal on the Map is rather small, just $1,000. It's intended to help those who've never saved before get into the habit of putting a small amount of their income aside in an emergency fund. You have to start somewhere, and the idea is to achieve a short-term goal while establishing good savings habits and building confidence.

As the Map progresses, the goals for that emergency fund increase, from $1,000 to one month's living expenses, then three months. This, obviously, is not an overnight process, and it's understood that it will take the average individual or family from one to three years to achieve just those preliminary savings goals. After the emergency account is "fully funded," believers are encouraged to begin saving for major purchases, such as a home, children's education and retirement.

As you can see by those "normal" savings goals, the *Crown Money Map*® was designed for normal economic circumstances. It was our response to thousands of questions about personal finances from believers who needed help setting priorities and making tough decisions. The Map has served well the hundreds of thousands of people who use it. Certainly, if you were to obtain a copy today and follow each step faithfully, you would be miles ahead of the average family in the U.S. The average personal savings rate for Americans is now only 3.9% of gross income, not helped at all by the fact that average household credit card debt is well over $7,000.

It's frightening to see how the U.S. stacks up to other countries with regard to the average personal savings rates of income:

Personal Savings Rates - Global Ranking

CHINA	INDIA	TURKEY	SWITZERLAND	IRELAND	GERMANY	BRITAIN	BRAZIL	USA	JAPAN	AUSTRALIA
38%	34.7%	19.5%	14.3%	12.3%	11.7%	7%	6.8%	3.9%	2.8%	2.5%

Source: "How Household Savings Stack Up in Asia, the West, and Latin America," Bloomberg/Businessweek, June 10, 2010. http://www.businessweek.com/magazine/content/10_25/b4183010451928.htm

If you are currently using the *Crown Money Map®*, you've no doubt established saving and debt reduction habits that will be critical in the years ahead. So, don't throw away your Map, but simply modify your approach for a season as you implement The S.A.L.T. Plan™.

Perhaps God will lead us to avert this looming crisis as I outlined in the Four Economic Scenarios. During normal economic growth, simply saving for college, a home, or retirement is your biggest priority. However, as we see dark clouds looming on the horizon, we're going to have to take it to a whole new level.

If you haven't been using the *Crown Money Map*®, or haven't established a saving habit of any kind, you may find The S.A.L.T. Plan™ more challenging, but that is no reason to shrink from the task at hand. We're not expecting 100% perfection. Regardless of your income, debt levels or savings habits now, it is important that you begin to implement the plan in some fashion and do your best. An infant's first steps are tiny, but before you know it, the toddler is running around the house. It works the same way when you're developing new financial habits. Start with as much as you can, but don't worry if that is just a little. The goal is to prepare you for tough times ahead, and the more you prepare, the better equipped you'll be to weather the storms.

Save Like Joseph

Remember the first great famine we described earlier? After several years of famine, Joseph had taken all of the grain and livestock from the people. When the famine persisted, he took the people themselves as slaves. Do you remember how he kept them from starving?

"Joseph said to the people, 'Now that I have bought you and your land today for Pharaoh, here is seed for you so you can plant the ground. But when the crop comes in, give a fifth of it to Pharaoh. The other four-fifths you may keep as seed for the fields and as food for yourselves and your households and your children.'" [2]

Again, we see that this was the government, through a tax, implementing a savings program for the people. Joseph ensured that enough grain would be in the Pharaoh's storehouses to feed the people when all other resources failed them.

I told you before that this is not the typical biblical approach to saving—that is, waiting for the government to do it for you. In

[2] Genesis 47:23-24

The S.A.L.T. Plan™, you will do the saving. You will not wait for the government to save for you. It is always God's will that you rely on Him to provide through the resources He gives you—not the government. There is another extremely important lesson regarding saving that we can draw from this example, and that relates to the amount of saving. In Joseph's case, it was one-fifth, or 20%.

I do not believe God simply chose that amount arbitrarily. I believe it is His intention that in times of extreme danger, His people should set aside that proportion of their income. This, then, is the savings goal of the S.A.L.T. Plan™—20% of the income that God provides for you. I know that sounds drastic, perhaps even desperate, but I believe we must prepare for desperate times ahead.

Further, we must save 20% of our income for seven years, as did Joseph. If you were to achieve that goal, you would then have a full 140% of your income in savings of one form or another, and most likely, several.

Now, when I describe this goal to ardent followers of Crown's prior teaching on saving, the reaction is usually, "140%!? I thought it was three months' living expenses. Or six months, max. You can't be serious!"

I'm absolutely serious. Instead of three or six months, I'm saying that to weather the kind of storm we see looming on the economic horizon, you will need 16 to 18 months of income in savings. If you think this is way over the top, too extreme and completely unrealistic and unnecessary, let me give you just one current economic fact that should change your mind. Look closely at the table on the next page.

Unemployed people by duration of unemployment

	Less than 5 weeks	5 to 14 weeks	15 weeks +	15 to 26 weeks	27 weeks +	Average duration in weeks [1]	Median duration in weeks
NOT SEASONALLY ADJUSTED							
Sept 2010	2,830	3,127	8,133	2,075	6,108	34.1	20.5
Aug 2011	2,635	3,377	7,997	1,958	6,038	39.7	20.6
Sept 2011	2,760	2,726	8.034	1,816	6,217	41.0	22.2
SEASONALLY ADJUSTED							
Sept 2010	1,816	3,329	8,517	1,816	6,153	33.4	20.5
May 2011	1,964	2,892	8,184	1,964	6,200	39.7	22.0
June 2011	1,836	2,972	8,125	1,836	6,289	39.9	22.5
July 2011	1,965	3,088	8,150	1,965	6,185	40.4	21.5
Aug 2011	2,239	3,050	8,273	2,239	6,034	40.3	21.8
Sept 2011	2,086	2,904	8,328	2,086	6,242	40.5	22.2

Source: Bureau of Labor Statistics, U.S. Department of Labor

As of this writing, the average length of unemployment in the United States is just over 40 weeks. That's nine months! Moreover, that's only the average. Today it is not unusual for someone to be out of work for a year and a half, or more. In fact, you probably know one or more people who have been without work for that period, or even longer. Keep in mind; this is under our current precarious circumstances, not what we might expect in the event of an economic disaster of biblical proportions. Suddenly, 18 months of living expenses doesn't sound extreme at all, does it? In fact, it seems only prudent.

Some of you have been wise savers for many years, and may have achieved this benchmark already. But if not, don't be discouraged.

Saving is a defensive strategy. If you are married, this should be the responsibility of the person in the family best suited to the task. If you have trouble saving, the task begins with prayer. Humbly ask the Lord to give you the fruit of His Spirit—self-control.

"But the fruit of the Spirit is love, joy, peace, patience, kindness, goodness, faithfulness, gentleness and self-control. Against such things there is no law. Those who belong to Christ Jesus have crucified the sinful nature with its passions and desires." [3]

So the goal of your savings program should be 20% of your income for seven years, or a total of 140% of annual income. That should give you 16 to 18 months of living expenses in cash available for immediate access.

To achieve this, I recommend dividing your income as shown in the graphic below to prepare you for an economic event of biblical proportions. Keep in mind that this model will not harm you, and in fact is highly beneficial, even if we somehow manage to avert such an event.

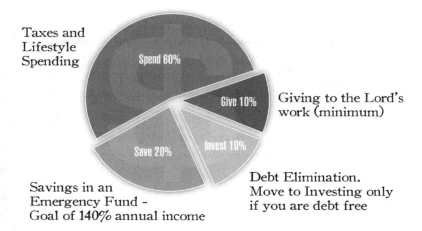

Taxes and Lifestyle Spending

Spend 60%

Give 10%

Giving to the Lord's work (minimum)

Save 20%

Invest 10%

Savings in an Emergency Fund - Goal of 140% annual income

Debt Elimination. Move to Investing only if you are debt free

[3] Galatians 5:22-24

If you are currently not saving anything, obviously you will need to make a 20% adjustment in your lifestyle to achieve a 20% surplus. If you're not saving and giving anything to your church, you will need to make at least a 30% reduction in your lifestyle.

I cannot emphasize strongly enough the absolute importance of remaining generous to God's Kingdom while implementing The S.A.L.T. Plan™. The 10% directed toward giving, by the way, is only the minimum. I encourage you to give as much as you can during the process and be prepared to give even more during a crisis.

Developing a Saving Mindset

Throughout the Great Depression and on into World War II, there was a common expression in America: *"Use it Up, Wear it Out. Make it Do, or Do Without."*

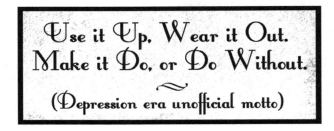

Back then, there was no stigma attached to living a frugal lifestyle. To the contrary, frugality was considered a virtue. To the extent that the term "consumer" existed in the popular lexicon, it was certainly not considered a good thing. That saving mindset of the 1930s and '40s was a far cry from today's *"Buy it Now, Throw it Out. Buy a New One, Don't Go Without."*

In order to save 20% of your income, you may need to lower your expenses by dramatically re-ordering your lifestyle. While it might seem difficult, I assure you this is not rocket science. It's okay to start out slow, perhaps trying one thing to reduce your expenses. As you achieve success, your confidence will grow and you will be willing to take on new challenges. Remember the adage "How do you eat an elephant? —One bite at a time!"

Tips for living on less:

1. Plant a garden and begin to grow some of your own food. Learn how to can the surplus. This is a great project to involve the kids in your new lifestyle.

2. Carry a small note pad or index card with you at all times. Write down every expenditure. Do this as a couple if you are married. At the end of the day/week/month, compile the expenditures in categories so you know where the money is going. Continue this habit until you have control of spontaneous, non-essential expenses.

3. Learn to wait 30 days before any major purchase and to shop for a bargain on every purchase.

4. Spend less on utilities: adjust the thermostat to be a little uncomfortable or turn it off and open the windows; take shorter showers; carry your garbage to the landfill instead of paying for a service.

5. Bundle your trips so that you drive less; shop for best prices on gasoline.

6. Join a food co-op or buy a warehouse membership; buy in bulk items you frequently use.

7. Learn to need less entertainment. Cable TV, Internet, movies, iTunes, sports events and eating out are expensive forms of entertainment that can be eliminated and replaced with trips to the library, a walk in the park, a picnic with friends or family as you develop an appreciation for less noise and more beauty.

8. Buy used; shop at thrift stores and garage sales. Check for items on Craigslist and eBay from reputable sellers.

9. Learn to make things yourself that you once thought you had to purchase such as clothes, gifts, cards, meals and treats.

10. Don't pay for services that you can do yourself, such as taxes, maintenance, cleaning and home improvement projects. Check out "How To" manuals from the library and sign up for free classes to learn new skills at home improvement stores.

11. Think differently: Ask yourself, "How can I get this done for less? What would I do if I had no money to pay for this but still needed it? Who do I know that may have advice or resources to help me with this need? What can I exchange or barter to get what I need?"

12. Clear your mind: Walk more, ride a bike, cancel magazine subscriptions and stop watching television commercials that create a desire for more things.

But don't stop there! You can comb the Internet for more ways to cut your expenses. And while you're at it, don't forget about the big expenditures.

See if you can refinance your automobile loan to a lower interest rate. Unlike with a mortgage, there are no closing costs when you re-fi your car loan! Also, check around for a lower quote on your auto insurance.

If you begin to adopt a saving mindset, you'll soon find that you actually have surplus cash. Now the question is where do you put it?

Best Methods for Saving Cash

Now that you have surplus money in your budget, start an automatic savings deposit directly from your paycheck each pay period into a savings account—preferably one that you don't see regularly, perhaps even at a separate bank. This is easy to set up with online banking.

Always keep one full month of income at home in a fire-proof safe placed in an out of the way location. No sense making it easy for thieves in the event of a burglary. This is somewhat controversial, but I can't tell you the peace of mind it will give you to know that you can operate for an entire month in the event of a catastrophic banking emergency.

Other tips for squeezing money out of your spending cycle and into savings:

• Start a jar for pocket change.

• Keep all budgeted, discretionary money in cash and divide it into envelopes, stored in your safe.

- Keep a copy of your spending plan in your wallet or purse at all times, or

- Sign up for Crown Mvelopes at Crown.Mvelopes.com.

- Before you buy anything, shop for the best deals online. Often you can find better deals online than in stores on everyday items such as diapers, furnace filters and even coffee.

- Use a personal reward system to celebrate your progress. There is great joy in something as simple as an ice cream cone when you know you've earned it.

- Have a circle of friends join you in your drive to save so you can share ideas and keep each other encouraged.

A Word about Banks

Put money only in a bank that is insured by the Federal Deposit Insurance Corporation (FDIC) or a credit union insured by the NCUA. However, the banking crisis of 2008 showed us that even with federally insured accounts, complications can arise that temporarily put your funds off limits. Even though your money is "safe," it may require paperwork and time to get your hands on it in the event of a bank failure, however unlikely that may be.

You've heard the saying, "Don't put all of your eggs in one basket." The same applies to your emergency savings. Distribute those funds into at least two if not more completely separate banks. That way you will always have access to a portion of your funds.

Should you manage to accrue $250,000 in a savings account, please take heed of the following from the FDIC:

"The FDIC insures deposits that a person holds in one insured bank separately from any deposits that the person owns in another separately chartered insured bank. For example, if a person has a certificate of deposit at Bank A and has a certificate of deposit at Bank B, the accounts would each be insured separately up to $250,000. Funds deposited in separate branches of the same insured bank are not separately insured." [4]

And that's why you need to use more than one bank. Even though funds held in separate savings classes in the same bank are insured above $250,000, a safe rule would be to never keep more than $250,000 in a single bank. If you're anything like me that will never be a problem!

It is possible for the unthinkable to happen, and that is the failure of the FDIC program. Alternatives to commercial bank accounts are placing your savings in credit unions or simply keeping them in your physical possession in a water-proof, fire-proof, security safe.

You can also check out the financial condition of most banks and savings institutions online. Bankrate.com has an excellent 5-star rating system on banks, thrifts and credit unions. [5]

---

[4] "FDIC Insurance Coverage Basics," Federal Deposit Insurance Corporation, Aug., 22, 2011. http://www.fdic.gov/deposit/deposits/insured/basics.html

[5] "Bank Ratings for Thrift, Credit Union and National Banks," http://www.bankrate.com/rates/safe-sound/bank-ratings-search.aspx

The Ladder Method for Certificate of Deposits

The Ladder Method for managing CDs is an excellent idea. Let's say you have saved up $5,000 and you want to move it from your savings account into CDs. At your bank (or banks!) you buy a single CD in each of one-, two-, three-, four- and five-year term increments. A year from now, when the first CD matures, you simply put that money into a new, five-year CD. Do this each year as a CD matures, reinvesting the money into another new five-year CD. Your bank can help you through the process.

This method has been shown in most cases to give a slightly higher overall return on your cash as you have portions of your savings in a variety of CDs ranging from long-term maturities that tend to pay higher returns to short-term CDs that pay very low returns but are available much more readily.

As the money you hold in CDs grows, you will be sorely tempted to put it into higher risk, higher return investments. Read carefully, because this is important: Do not invest this money! Investment money is at risk. These funds need to be kept at your disposal, where the worst that can happen is you pay an early withdrawal penalty should you need cash before a CD matures.

After achieving 140% of your gross annual income for emergency savings, you can then begin to move excess funds into investment assets.

If You Have Debt

"Just as the rich rule the poor, so the borrower is servant to the lender." [6]

Obviously, debt is going to slow down your savings program, so it can't be ignored. My advice is to divert half of your surplus income into savings and half toward paying off any consumer debt you may have, such as credit cards and car loans. When your consumer debt is retired, you can then put 100% of your surplus cash into savings.

Use the ***Debt Snowball Method*** to pay off your debt in the shortest time possible. (See charts below)

Debt Snowball Method

Debt Repayment Plan at 1 Month

		Entry Columns			Calculated Columns	
#	Creditor	Principal Balance ($)	Interest Rate (%)	Payment Amount ($)	Interest Cost	# of Pmts Left
A	PAID					
B	Sears	204	23	204		1
C	Visa	1,184	14	30		54
D	Mastercard	3,583	21	86	3,542.00	89
E	Student Loan	10,896	5	150	2,155.00	87
F	Auto Loan	19,526	6	350	3,523.00	66
G	Mortgage	141,521	5.25	1100	67,618.00	190
H						
I						
J						

Pay Additional Amount to Next Payee(s)

Total Payment Per Month: $1,920.00

[6] Proverbs 22:7

Simply make minimum payments on all of your outstanding debts, except for the one with the highest interest rate (Debt A). Use all of your remaining debt reduction funds each month to make the maximum payment possible on Debt A. Continue to do this each month until Debt A is gone.

Debt Repayment Plan at 2 Months

#	Creditor	Principal Balance ($)	Interest Rate (%)	Payment Amount ($)	Interest Cost	# of Pmts Left
A	PAID PAID					
B	PAID PAID					
C	Visa	1,168	14	30	28.00	52
D	Mastercard	3,564	21	290	3,542.00	88
E	Student Loan	10,791	5	150	2,155.00	86
F	Auto Loan	19,274	6	350	3,523.00	65
G	Mortgage	141,040	5.25	1100	67,618.00	189
H						
I						
J						

Entry Columns — *Calculated Columns*

Total Payment Per Month: $1,920.00

Then, take the amount you had been paying on Debt A and add it each month to the minimum payment on the next highest interest rate debt (Debt B).

When Debt B is retired, add that amount each month to the minimum payment on Debt C until it is paid off. Remember to maintain minimum payments on all of your other debts!

As each debt is paid off, add your newly available funds to

pay down the next highest interest rate debt until all of your debt is gone. The process starts out slowly, but gains speed as you continue to faithfully pay off your debts—hence the term "snowball method." Obviously, you must stop all borrowing in order for the process to work as quickly as possible.

Longer term debt, such as student loans and your mortgage, is another story. Obviously, you can't wait until your mortgage is paid off to begin saving for an economic event of biblical proportions. Continue making minimum payments on these obligations as you build your savings.

I realize that advising you not to make extra payments on your mortgage is somewhat controversial, especially in light of Crown's previous teaching to the contrary. However, let's not forget our goal. We are preparing you to have maximum liquid assets on hand. That cash will enable you to pay your mortgage should you experience a loss of income as a result of an extreme economic emergency. A smaller principal amount on your mortgage does you no good if you have no way of making your monthly payment.

I do, however, advise you to pay off your student loans and mortgage before you begin to invest monies that you've accrued beyond your 140% of annual income (which you will continue to hold in savings). The exception to this is with a qualified retirement program in which your employer makes matching contributions. In that event, you should continue to invest up to the level of your employer's maximum contribution. It is, after all, free money. However, be sure you are managing and supervising the performance of the funds that are invested in your company retirement program. In times of great distress, you must be vigilant to monitor all banks and retirement programs regardless of their past history.

CHAPTER TEN

10

A = ASSET ALLOCATION

"Give portions to seven, yes to eight, for you do not know what disaster may come upon the land."

- Ecclesiastes 11:2

Solomon's Diversification Method

In 2001, the United States was rocked by the Enron Scandal. Nearly 5,600 people lost their jobs after the $100 billion energy company filed for bankruptcy. Stockholders lost $60 billion when the price of shares plummeted, and Enron employees lost more than $2 billion in retirement savings held in Enron stocks.[1]

Prior to the fall of Enron, the company had performed so well that many of those Enron employees held the vast majority of their retirement funds in the company's stocks, against common sense. No matter how well a single asset is performing, you should never trust it with the bulk of your savings or investments.

As of this writing, it is estimated that some 25 million Americans are unemployed or under-employed, that is, holding either part-time or full-time jobs that pay less than the employee's experience and training should command during a strong economy.

As noted earlier, the average amount of time a person remains unemployed is now approximately nine months. Clearly, one's income cannot be taken for granted.

For all of these reasons, what I call "Solomon's Diversification Method" involves your savings (and investments) and your income. Both are critical assets that must be allocated wisely to protect them from the consequences of a major economic event.

Solomon tells us to "give portions" to seven or eight. I don't believe

[1] "The Enron Effect," *Time*, May 28, 2006. http://www.time.com/time/magazine/article/0,9171,1198917,00.html

this is intended to be a precise number, but instead conveys the notion of dividing up your assets into many different classes which react differently to market forces. This principle means that you should avoid having any more than 12% to15% of your total assets in any one investment. When the value of one investment suffers, the value of another may increase, or at least be less likely to lose value at the same rate as the others.

Let's begin, then, with the definition of an asset. It is simply anything with a positive economic value—an acre of land, an automobile (owned outright), the balance in a savings account, an annuity, or the cash value of an insurance policy. Your labor, or more precisely the income that it produces, could also be considered an asset.

Diversification of Investments

Saving and investing are not interchangeable terms. The difference between saving and investing is that saving involves little, if any, risk to your money. The potential for a return on your money is always directly related to the level of risk involved. Therefore, your federally insured savings account pays very little interest. Its true value is reflected in its security.

Investing, on the other hand, puts your money at risk. You should never invest money that you can't afford to lose. This is why the prudent investor moves money away from stocks toward more secure instruments as retirement nears.

As we learned from our analysis of the biblical famines, there will always be those who profit during difficult times. And for those who have investable assets, there will always be investors seeking to protect their assets.

Invested money is put to work to make a return and thus must be at risk of loss to capture a gain. I am not a qualified investment advisor; therefore, consider seeking investment advice from a professional who shares your biblical worldview before making any investment decisions.

No one knows the future, no matter how much they may try to convince you. We do not know if an economic event of biblical proportions will bring about inflation or deflation or both in the years ahead.

Inflation occurs when prices rise; deflation, when prices fall. Your investing diversification options should be based on the current price environment—inflation or deflation.

Diversification of Investments

- Different asset classes/sectors
- Allocations vary according to risk tolerance
- Seek professional advice

If you have assets now, these should be properly allocated into diversified sectors of the economy. This is a sample of diversification.

Diversification of Income

"Sow your seed in the morning, and at evening let not your hands be idle, for you do not know which will succeed, whether this or that, or whether both will do equally well." [2]

This verse recommends that one person should have two incomes. Do you have a secondary skill or interest that could provide additional income? It can be completely unrelated to your regular employment. Everyone has interests, hobbies or skills that could be a potential source of revenue if made into a business. In the past, this has been referred to as "moonlighting" meaning working after the sun has set.

Or, you could diversify your income by finding additional outlets for your primary skillset. Perhaps you are an accountant or a graphic designer with a full-time job. You may be able to pick up additional money freelancing in the evenings or on weekends. The current job market, with increased emphasis on part-time and contract employment, may actually make this easier than in times past. A contemporary term for this is "giganomics" or having a number of part-time "gigs" to create a full-time income.

A family business is also a great way to provide multiple incomes. Consider starting a small business on the side to involve your spouse and children. You can work your regular job by day, and become an entrepreneur by night. For the best Christian advice on setting up a home-based business, you can't do better than Wade Myers. Explore all of his resources at Crown.org.

We all have special gifts and talents. The best investment you can make is to develop them to your utmost for use in your regular job or business. This should be a higher priority than passive investments.

---

[2] Ecclesiastes 11:6

Remember that a "secure job" is being paid a wage in exchange for the hours that you work. If you are able to give up the security of a regular salary, the risk you take will enable you to earn the profits from your labor as opposed to a guaranteed salary. Ideally, taking this risk should provide a greater reward in exchange for your labor.

Diversifying for Inflation

In an inflationary scenario, prices rise. Investors who diversify for this scenario generally divide their assets as follows:

- Gold, precious metals and commodities in general. The prices for this asset class typically will rise during times of inflation.

- Energy and oil sectors. These are essential to the global economy and generally do very well in times of inflation.

- Technology. Regardless of inflation or deflation, new technologies will emerge and be in demand.

- Emerging markets. Stocks tied to foreign countries experiencing broad and rapid growth rise during inflationary periods.

- Avoid leveraged companies. Stay away from companies that borrow heavily or lend heavily to others.

- Avoid excessive assets in fixed income vehicles such as bonds (unless you're nearing retirement). Typically, fixed income vehicles underperform in an inflationary environment.

- Avoid staying in cash. Inflation means your currency is losing cash value every day.

Diversifying for Deflation

In a deflationary scenario, prices fall. Investors who diversify for this scenario generally divide their assets as follows:

- Fixed income instruments such as bonds, which are considered safe in deflationary times.

- Technology which are normally in demand regardless of inflation or deflation.

- Avoid stocks. Deflation has severe effects on most companies, resulting in reduced profit margins.

- Avoid gold and precious metals. They generally perform poorly in a deflationary period, except in the most extreme cases of a currency collapse.

- Avoid real estate investments. The housing market suffered as a result of the subprime collapse. The result was a significant loss of property value. Renting is a better option than owning in a deflationary environment.

- Avoid emerging markets. Deflation has a bigger impact on developing economies. Prices fall faster and companies suffer more in developing nations than in established markets.

A Few General Principles for Allocating Assets

- Preserving cash is the very best strategy to maintain mobility in the event of bank failures, a collapse in the credit markets or government defaulting on its debt. Consider having some cash in currencies other than the dollar.

- Short- and long-term bonds are considered a necessary portion of every portfolio but do your homework. Don't trust rating agencies.

- High quality dividend paying stocks typically provide good returns for the long term investor.

- Consider becoming a lender. The Bible warns against borrowing, but does not prohibit being a lender so long as you do not charge excessive interest rates. Consider peer to peer lending as a part of your portfolio.

- If you do not understand the basics of investing, I strongly urge you to seek professional help from a trusted advisor with a biblical worldview before you put money at risk.

- Allow the Lord to guide you as to the appropriate time to seek gain or to remove your money from risk. Remember that no man knows the future, so avoid trying to time the market by going in when it is low and getting out when it is high. Long-term investment strategies have proven to be superior to market timing strategies.

"Be sure you know the condition of your flocks, give careful attention to your herds; for riches do not endure forever, and a crown is not secure for all generations." [3]

Food and Water: Key Commodities

My dad was raised during the Great Depression. He lived through some very hard times in rural Texas and he never forgot those lessons. To this day, he reminds me of a few considerations that shaped his family's thinking during those extremely difficult times. Their primary considerations were access to water and food.

[3] Proverbs 27:23-24

When buying a house, he always wanted to know how far it was to the nearest lake or creek to get access to water. He never assumed that tap water would be available or affordable.

These days, almost everyone has city water. But can you imagine not having enough cash to pay your water bill? In the United States, we take water for granted. I'm not saying we should expect a lengthy interruption of municipal water services, but knowing how you would obtain water in such an event is wise. In the South, outdoor watering restrictions are commonplace. How much more strain on water systems would it take for this precious commodity to become rationed?

If you own property and can afford to put in your own well, it's something to consider. It would certainly be a way around those troublesome restrictions. Perhaps you and your neighbors could share the expense of the well.

For many reasons, I think it is also wise to learn how to grow your own food. Without a sufficient supply of water, that is practically impossible. It doesn't take much land to get started. You'd be surprised at how much food can be produced from a tiny plot in the back yard, a few pots on the deck, or even a window box. Lack of knowledge is a far greater limitation than lack of space. Remember, the idea is to produce abundant resources that will provide not only your family's needs, but that can also be shared with others to demonstrate the love of Christ.

"Who then is the faithful and wise servant, whom the master has put in charge of the servants in his household to give them their food at the proper time? It will be good for that servant whose master finds him doing so when he returns. I tell you the truth, he will put him in charge of all his possessions." [4]

We've all seen news footage of empty shelves in stores when a

[4] Matthew 24:45-47

winter storm interrupts food deliveries for a day or two or the panic of an approaching hurricane drives people to stock their pantries. What would happen in the event those trucks were delayed by weeks, or even months?

God's Word tells us that food is the key commodity in difficult times. In the years ahead, I believe we must become far more intentional about ensuring access to food and clean water. It's only prudent to develop a strategy to safeguard abundant supplies of these vitally important commodities.

Here are some ideas:

- **Plant** a garden. Learn to grow food in a raised bed in your backyard.

- **Grow** extra food in pots on the balcony of your apartment or back patio.

- **Stock up** on supplies of seed and non-perishable items.

- **Keep a water filter** in your home.

- **Know** where you can draw water from a well or local supply.

- **Learn** to can extra produce like fruit and vegetables.

- **Sell** excess food at a local Farmer's Market.

- **Find recipes** for stretching your food budget.

- **Learn** to consume less at each meal.

- **Make** casseroles and freeze them.

- **Freeze** common items like waffles and chili.

- **Participate** in a co-op for farm fresh eggs, milk and meat.

- **Raise** chickens, goats or cattle if you have access to land.

- **Learn** to hunt and/or fish for your food.

I've read of hunters who don't particularly like to eat what they kill, but instead give away meat to needy families. I think this is a perfect example of allocating one's assets and resources (hunting skills in this case) to witness for Christ. What skills or resources do you have that could be used in the same way in a time of crisis? By the way, you don't have to wait for a crisis to begin sharing your resources.

Food Preparedness

People have stockpiled food since Adam and Eve were shown the Garden gate. It's only in modern times and mostly in the western developed nations that we take food for granted. As a result, we keep very little of it on hand, never much more than a few days' worth. After all, we rarely experience even a hiccup in the food delivery system here in the U.S. If that were to change, however, few of us would be prepared to go more than a week before experiencing hunger.

The human body needs three main nutritional components: carbohydrates, proteins and fats. Carbs are readily converted into sugars and provide needed energy. Proteins primarily enable the body to preserve and build muscle. Despite the hysteria of recent years about the evil of fats, they are necessary. Without getting into the debate about good and bad fats, suffice it to say that fats provide essential fatty acids that the body needs to function, right down to something so basic as cell membrane production. Here's a checklist of things to keep in your emergency food pantry. Your goal is to stockpile enough food to sustain your household for one month or longer.

- **Dried or canned meats, canned fish**—good sources of protein with a long shelf-life

- **Dried or canned beans** for carbs and protein

- **Canned fruits and vegetables**

- **Dried fruits**—consider purchasing a food dehydrator to make your own

- **Nuts** are perfect emergency foods with protein, fats and some carbs plus a long shelf life

Start adding to this list with ideas of your own. Just make sure that the foods in your pantry provide one or more of proteins, fats and carbs and have a long shelf life.

Here are a few other essential items to keep on hand:

- **Water**—it's rare, but water systems can be contaminated by storms or a breakdown in purification systems. In 1993, the Milwaukee, Wisconsin municipal water system became infected with Cryptosporidium, killing 47 people and sickening at least 400,000 others. Officials have long feared that municipal water systems could be targeted by terrorists. Always keep a few days' worth of bottled water on hand.

- **Multivitamins** to make sure you are getting all essential vitamins and minerals

- **Several can openers**—these simple devices often break easily and you don't want to be without one

- **A camping stove with fuel source** in case of gas or electrical interruption

- **Flashlights, batteries and matches**

Your goal is to have a month's worth of provisions for your household. Once you've achieved that, continue to build on these resources so that you have a surplus to share with others. That, after all, is what The S.A.L.T. Plan™ is all about.

CHAPTER ELEVEN

11

L = LIQUIDITY

L iquidity is the ultimate attribute in preparedness. Too often, we are trapped by events because our assets and our lives are invested in ways that are not liquid. Or, our hearts are so attached to our possessions that we cannot leave them behind if the need arises.

We're taught to make investments for the long term, but we never think about what we would do in the short term if we had to become liquid. In The S.A.L.T. Plan™, liquidity not only means that you can convert fixed assets into transferrable assets; it means that *everything* can be mobile.

In modern day market terminology, of course, liquidity is the ability to easily convert an asset to cash or cash equivalent.

Generally, liquid assets give a lower rate of return than savings or investments that tie up your money for a longer period of time. Part of the risk of higher return investments is that often they are not easily converted into safer holdings as conditions change. Rental property, a small business or a rare coin collection are examples of items that may not be very liquid in a crisis.

It is sometimes said in investing that getting a return on your money isn't as important as *getting your money returned.* The assurance of having quick access to your money is the essence of the safe, liquid asset.

Liquidity is also known as "marketability," meaning there is a ready market for your asset—someone willing to buy it for cash.

In biblical terms, however, we often see that liquidity is simply being available, unhindered and mobile to answer God's calling. Imagine leaving everything you feel is safe and comfortable, as the Lord commanded Abram:

"The Lord had said to Abram, 'Leave your country, your people and your father's household and go to the land I will show you. I will make you into a great nation and I will bless you; I will make your name great, and you will be a blessing.'" [1]

At the age of 75, Abram set out and traveled as the Lord led him for what must have been a considerable time. Liquidity allowed Abram to be mobile—a very good thing as we see a little later in this passage:

"Now there was a famine in the land, and Abram went down to Egypt to live there for a while because the famine was severe." [2]

Liquidity, seen as mobility, is no less important today in the event of a major crisis. Consider the following possibilities that may require you to be more liquid or mobile:

- Lack of jobs or work in your area
- Rising crime
- God's calling you to take on a new mission
- Ability to support your family during hardship
- Need for closer proximity to a like-minded community of believers
- Persecution
- Changes in your health
- The need to lower your cost of living
- A desire for a change in lifestyle
- Closer proximity to fresh water, sunshine and land
- A move to a foreign country for a job or missionary work

[1] Genesis 12:1-2
[2] Genesis 12:10

In Genesis, we see how Abram handled many of the events that we may face in the future.

Persecution at the hands of government:

"Then Pharaoh gave orders about Abram to his men, and they sent him on his way, with his wife and everything he had. So Abram went up from Egypt to the Negev, with his wife and everything he had, and Lot went with him." [3]

Change in circumstances:

"So Abram said to Lot, 'Let's not have any quarreling between you and me, or between your herders and mine, for we are close relatives. Is not the whole land before you? Let's part company. If you go to the left, I'll go to the right; if you go to the right, I'll go to the left.'" [4]

Crime:

"When Abram heard that his relative had been taken captive, he called out the 318 trained men born in his household and went in pursuit as far as Dan." [5]

Surrendering our most precious possessions in obedience to God:

"When they reached the place God had told him about, Abraham built an altar there and arranged the wood on it. He bound his son Isaac and laid him on the altar, on top of the wood. Then he reached out his hand and took the knife to slay his son. But the angel of the Lord called out to him from heaven, 'Abraham! Abraham!'

---

[3] Genesis 12:20 – 13:1
[4] Genesis 13:8-9
[5] Genesis 14:14

'Here I am,' he replied.

'Do not lay a hand on the boy,' he said. 'Do not do anything to him. Now I know that you fear God, because you have not withheld from me your son, your only son.'" [6]

Here are some ways to be "liquid"—ready and responsive to a changing environment:

- Be sure you have "thrown off everything that hinders."

- Remove your security from money and possessions and anchor your identity in your eternal citizenship.

- Consider your current situation in light of these questions:

  - Would I be better off renting a home rather than owning it?

  - Would my business be better off if I rented an office or worked from home?

  - If God asked me to relocate, what would prevent me from obeying?

  - Do my investments need to be reallocated for better marketability?

  - Can I go "wherever and whenever" God may call me?

  - Do I have a passport?

  - Do I know a foreign language?

We see then that keeping our lives liquid is the opposite of having a "bunker mentality." It's difficult to move when you're underground, worried only about your own survival.

We've looked at Savings, Asset Allocation and Liquidity. You

---

[6] Genesis 22:9-12

now have a much better understanding of what it will take to be prepared for an economic event of biblical proportions. All of your preparations, however, will come to nothing unless they are bathed in the final component of The S.A.L.T. Plan™—Truth.

CHAPTER TWELVE

12

T = TRUTH

So far, we have covered the S.A.L. portions of The S.A.L.T. Plan™, which have been all about our physical preparation for an economic event of biblical proportions. Those components are certainly important as they prepare us for circumstances in this life.

The final element, however, Truth, has value not only in this life, but in the life to come. If we omit the Truth from our plan, we miss our opportunity to become the salt that God wants us to be for His glory.

"If you point these things out to the brothers and sisters, you will be a good minister of Christ Jesus, nourished on the truths of the faith and of the good teaching that you have followed. Have nothing to do with godless myths and old wives' tales; rather, train yourself to be godly. For physical training is of some value, but godliness has value for all things, holding promise for both the present life and the life to come." [1]

As you move forward then in your preparations, cling to the following biblical truths:

1. Take care of your family first, then others.

"If anyone does not provide for his relatives, and especially for his immediate family, he has denied the faith and is worse than an unbeliever." [2]

To prepare for very difficult times God commands us to view our family as our first responsibility. Once they are taken care of, we then are in a position to serve others. We see in 1 Kings 18 that when Ahab persecuted God's people, Obadiah provided food and water to 100 of God's prophets. We can assume from this that he held a high position in the government which allowed him to not only care for his own family but also many others. He avoided a

---

[1] 1 Timothy 4:6-8
[2] 1 Timothy 5:8

"bunker mentality" and was living for God's purposes.

2. Righteousness is the greatest protection in every circumstance. Read the Psalms and Proverbs and underline the promises to the righteous man/woman.

Here are just a few:

a. Psalm 34:19: *"A righteous man may have many troubles, but the Lord delivers him from them all..."*

b. Psalm 37:16: *"Better the little that the righteous have than the wealth of many wicked..."*

c. Psalm 55:22: *"Cast your cares on the Lord and he will sustain you; he will never let the righteous fall."*

d. Proverbs 10:21: *"The lips of the righteous nourish many, but fools die for lack of judgment."*

e. Proverbs 10:25: *"When the storm has swept by, the wicked are gone, but the righteous stand firm forever."*

f. Proverbs 11:28: *"Whoever trusts in his riches will fall, but the righteous will thrive like a green leaf."*

3. Wisdom is of greater value than gold.

"How much better to get wisdom than gold, to choose understanding rather than silver!" [3]

Many who read this will be unprepared for a severe economic crisis. You may lack the S., A. and L. of The S.A.L.T. Plan™, but you will always have God's wisdom. Don't despair; God will protect and keep you. His wisdom will never fail you. Invest your time

---

[3] Proverbs 16:16

and energy in gaining godly wisdom for the decisions you face.

4. God is the only true security in life.

> *"Never will I leave you; never will I forsake you. So we say with confidence, 'The Lord is my helper; I will not be afraid What can man do to me?'"* [4]

A crisis brings about the end of false security. It should not be a time of fear but of faith. When traditional support structures crumble, recognize that nothing can separate you from the love of God—not famine, nor persecution, or even death.

5. A financial crisis of biblical proportions will be the greatest opportunity for the advancement of God's kingdom.

> *"Whenever God slew them, they would seek him; they eagerly turned to him again."* [5]

Many believe that if the economy recovers it will lead the nation to a revival. This concept is contrary to Scripture. God warns that prosperity causes man to forget God, while suffering causes man to identify his need for God.

6. Some will panic and spread fear like a wildfire; even God's people will be tested. Others will be devoted to God as His steadfast witnesses to the joy that comes from faith.

> *"But because my servant Caleb has a different spirit and follows me wholeheartedly, I will bring him into the land he went to, and his descendants will inherit it."* [6]

[4] Hebrews 13:5-6
[5] Psalm 78:34
[6] Numbers 14:24

7. God's plan is to meet our needs in a body of believers and for us to meet the needs of those He puts in our lives.

"Love must be sincere. Hate what is evil; cling to what is good. Be devoted to one another in love. Honor one another above yourselves. Never be lacking in zeal, but keep your spiritual fervor, serving the Lord. Be joyful in hope, patient in affliction, faithful in prayer. Share with the Lord's people who are in need. Practice hospitality."

"Bless those who persecute you; bless and do not curse. Rejoice with those who rejoice; mourn with those who mourn. Live in harmony with one another. Do not be proud, but be willing to associate with people of low position. Do not be conceited."

"Do not repay anyone evil for evil. Be careful to do what is right in the eyes of everyone. If it is possible, as far as it depends on you, live at peace with everyone. Do not take revenge, my dear friends, but leave room for God's wrath, for it is written: 'It is mine to avenge; I will repay,' says the Lord. On the contrary: 'If your enemy is hungry, feed him; if he is thirsty, give him something to drink. In doing this, you will heap burning coals on his head.'

"Do not be overcome by evil, but overcome evil with good." [7]

---

[7] Romans 12:9-21

POSTSCRIPT

The Enemy will never "waste a good crisis," so neither should God's people. We can turn adversity into advantage by loving others and leading them to God's Kingdom in their time of need.

The S.A.L.T. Plan™ is designed for individuals and families to live prepared for a worst case scenario and to seize the opportunity to be "salt and light" as God commands. It can also be adapted for businesses and entire churches. In fact, we strongly recommend this approach, in which individuals and families join together in larger organizations to help and support each other while implementing the various components of the plan.

Are you ready to commit to being salt and light in a darkening world? We certainly hope so, and we want to stay in contact with you during the process. Here's how you can do that:

- **Join us on crown.org/facebook**

- **Subscribe to *Handwriting on the Wall* - Free, weekly economic update at Crown.org/handwriting**

- **Subscribe to *Do Well*, Crown's quarterly magazine.**

- **Let us know your progress. Would you like to share your story to help inspire others?**

NOW THAT YOU KNOW
THESE THINGS, YOU WILL BE BLESSED
IF YOU DO THEM.

~ John 13:17

The S.A.L.T. Plan™
Q&A

Did you write *The S.A.L.T. Plan*™ because you think that Christians are unprepared?

Yes. The reason I felt compelled to develop this plan was to shock us out of our typical mindset. We tend to think everything will always get better. We are very optimistic people but that leads us to be unprepared for something unexpected. I was impacted by the events in Japan in March of 2011. They had an earthquake, a tsunami and a nuclear threat all at once. It was shocking to see the unthinkable actually happen.

I think we're like little orchids that have been growing under a sun lamp. If you place that beautiful orchid out on the front porch and the storms come, they just wilt. We're called to be like oak trees, capable of enduring massive storms.

Do you think that a global economic crisis is imminent?

Again, without being prophetic and saying I know what's going to happen and when it's going to happen, I just know what the Scripture says, that we should live in a state of readiness. I think that should be the mindset of the Christian, especially now.

Can anyone truly be prepared for such an overwhelming economic event?

I wrote the book thinking of something far worse than a simple recession or depression—an event of biblical proportions. It's like the 100-year flood when the Mississippi overflowed its banks. You're not talking about just a little heavy rain. That was an extraordinary flood. Yet, some farmers, businesses and families got prepared and put sandbags out themselves. They didn't wait on FEMA to do it. Because they were prudent and wise, they not only averted getting wiped out from the 100-year flood but were in a position to serve others who were not prepared.

Isn't a survivalist mentality wrong?

Yes, the modern survivalist mentality we see all around us is wrong. It's not the Christian mentality. And many of the Christians are thinking exactly like the world; that is, when we think of being prepared, it's similar to the plan than the survivalists have. That is not what I am trying to communicate here.

I've got friends who right now have the bunker plan—guns, ammunition and gold. They're ready for a personal all out survival of the fittest. They're not ready for *The S.A.L.T. Plan™* because the mindset is totally different when you are planning to help and serve others.

Will those who are prepared be spared from suffering?

That is a question only God can answer; however, in Matthew 25, we learn from the Parable of the Ten Virgins that as soon as they knew they needed oil in their lamps and didn't have it—it was too late. The parable is telling us that there will come a day when everyone in the world recognizes his or her need for Him. Since we know this now, we should be preparing to help others have "oil in their lamps."

Explain why you think people need to save 20% of their income. That seems like hoarding.

I take a strong lesson from the first great biblical famine that we need to save 20% of our income for 7 years, which means a total of 140% of our current income because the western governments have not saved any money. We should lead the way. When I shared this with a couple of friends they replied, "I thought it was 3 to 6 months! Why so much!?" One friend even said, "Forget it. There's no way."

Okay, you can argue with it, but if you don't think you can do it and you don't start, you won't. But it's "do-able" because it's proportional to your income. It's not like you must have a set amount like half a million dollars.

Don't be reliant upon someone else to save for you. And if you think our government's going to do it for you and be benevolent in a great crisis—that's a misplaced dependency. When it really gets tough, welfare programs may disappear.

Hoarding is when you stockpile money or supplies without any purpose other than meeting personal needs. The S.A.L.T. Plan™ calls for continual generosity of 10% or more and the ability to serve others when they are caught unprepared. That is what it means to be salt, to be a preservative during a severe trial or time of testing.

Do churches need to be thinking about their plans and budgets as well?

Yes, many churches need to think about adopting the same plan. Church after church after church will experience significant economic problems. The bigger ones are going to struggle more than the little ones because of their massive overhead and infrastructure. I think it's going to be more difficult for them, especially if they have debt.

When we talk about 20% savings, are we including IRAs and other retirement accounts?

The 20% savings of the S.A.L.T. Plan™ should be separate from retirement savings or money that is invested.

You should set aside 20% in cash or liquid savings for your emergency needs. This should be money that you have access to without a penalty. And you have to be careful because I think that in a severe downturn even the FDIC insurance program could become a problem. It is a mistake to have all of your savings in one bank if we have a crisis of biblical proportions.

Where should we put our money if not in US banks?

Mark Faber, the Austrian economist, recently said, "Diversification no longer means different asset classes; it should also mean diversification of your money into different governmental jurisdictions." He believes it is wise to consider accounts in safe countries like Australia, Singapore, Switzerland, and Canada.

Be very careful with offshore banks or putting money in countries with unstable governments.

What about my 401k, 403b, IRA or other investments in tax sheltered accounts?

If you've reached the age where your retirement assets have matured, you can cash them out without penalty and allocate those assets into this plan. However, I am not advising people to cash out now because the penalty is too great for most people to absorb. Be patient because your investments may continue to grow but also be very informed of market volatility. Don't let assets sit in accounts without your vigilant oversight.

If you are very young, less than 35, consider rolling your investments over into a Roth IRA now. You will need professional counsel to determine the financial benefits and impact of this decision. My opinion is that taxes will continue to increase over time and having a Roth IRA will likely yield the best returns as you make tax free withdrawals later.

If the US government proposes a federal annuity program for all retirement accounts, would it be wise for seniors to convert to this plan to guarantee some income?

This is happening in other countries and some members of the US Congress are considering right now. In exchange for your 401k, IRA or other qualified retirement program, the government will give you a guaranteed annuity of 4 to 4.5 % on that balance for the rest of your life. Here's the reason it looks so good: People are only getting .5% to 1% right now, so they think, "Four times as much! That sounds like a great deal!"

Here's the problem. What you are really getting is an I.O.U. The government takes possession of your cash and savings in exchange for a promise. There's about $15 trillion sitting in retirement funds right now. But I think we need to be wary of that plan, because what seems like an increase in security and a higher return is actually more dependence on the U.S. Government to manage the money properly. How has the government managed the resources we've given it so far? I think it is a poor decision that could potentially enslave millions of people.

For young people who may have just purchased a home, the 20% savings component may cause some confusion. Do they pay down the mortgage as quickly as possible, or save the cash? Is it either/or?

I would advise making your regular mortgage payments while you save your 20% of income for seven years. You can always apply this savings to your mortgage later if the economic horizon improves.

However, a lower principal amount on your mortgage will be small consolation if you have no income and your cash runs out, making it impossible to pay your mortgage.

If you are under financial stress now, consider selling your house, renting and starting an aggressive savings plan. This is an individual choice that must be led by the Lord after wise counsel and prayer since no one knows the future.

What about crime and social unrest? How do we prepare for that?

If you live in a large metropolitan area vulnerable to violent crime now, it is likely to get worse during a crisis. If you live in an area with low crime, it is likely to remain stable. However, this is a variable that should be considered in your Liquidity planning. Has God called you to be the salt and light in your area? Can you relocate in the event of a significant increase in crime in your area? What are the needs of your family? These must be considerations between you, your family and the Lord.

Why do you describe food and water as key commodities?

My dad was raised during the Great Depression. He said that his parents' perspective was to always have a personally sustainable lifestyle, i.e. a home that was paid for within close proximity to a clean water supply and enough of a yard to plant a garden. This was the common approach held by many who experienced the hardships of the time—to cover their basic needs and be able to survive without income.

What if I have none of these? Should we be digging wells and planting gardens?

I think if you have the ability to do that, it's a great idea. If not, develop a co-op with some friends or neighbors who can provide needed resources in exchange for labor or financial participation. Many will not have the knowledge to do this, but you can find others who do. One of my friends is a master gardener. He and his wife grow an enormous amount of food in their suburban backyard. They have taught us how to plant our own garden plus we buy products from them as needed. Other friends raise goats, chickens and cattle, plus they have a beekeeping operation. We buy eggs, honey and meat from them.

What about freeze dried food or bulk grain?

Freeze dried food is easy to store but very expensive while grain has an incredibly long shelf life and is relatively inexpensive. We buy grain and other items that come in large bags or five-gallon buckets. Every anniversary of 9/11, my wife, Ann, restocks items we may need. We spend about four times our normal monthly budget for the annual stock up of grains.

What about gasoline? Do we need to keep our own private supply?

Several years ago, we experienced a severe gasoline shortage in our area due to the impact of a hurricane on refineries in Texas. In some cases, people were driving for a half hour to locate any stations that had supply. Not only did rationing by the suppliers go into effect (no one could purchase more than 12 gallons per vehicle), but price gouging took place. However, storing gasoline is very risky. I think a better strategy is to have a low cost form of transportation that reduces your dependence on your car. Can you walk to work? Can you ride a bike or scooter to work? Can you form a car pool with co-workers? These are better strategies for a potential gas shortage.

Should people own guns and ammunition?

I am a supporter of our Second Amendment rights to own and bear arms. However, I think the purpose of owning a gun(s) should be two-fold: 1) learning to hunt for food as needed and 2) to provide security from violence. This second reason would be a rare and extreme case for the vast majority of people. The idea of building a fortress and developing an attitude of hostility towards others should be eliminated from the thinking of a Christian.

My pastor and I were discussing that as elders of the church, we've got to prepare our people for hard times. Do you agree that the Church should have this responsibility?

Absolutely. The Bible is full of examples of God's people helping one another during difficult times. Financial catastrophes may be the greatest opportunity the church has had to demonstrate the love of God.

There are two ways for a pastor to approach this. One is to draw lessons from the Great Depression, which is on people's minds right now. Many are wondering if we're going into another depression. It would be fascinating to have a townhall type meeting in churches to hear the lessons that seniors might be willing to share. Another method would be to lead the church through a Bible study analyzing times of crisis similar to what I have done looking at some of the great famines.

You talk a lot about liquidity and mobility? How important is it?

Liquidity is one of the highest forms of preparedness. Many people will get trapped during a surprise event because they're typically invested in ways that are not liquid. For instance, being upside down on your mortgage was a very poor decision that hurt millions of families when the real estate bubble burst.

Liquidity is great protection because it means that you can convert fixed assets into transferrable assets; it means that everything, including you as a person can be mobile. As a culture, we view our lives and lifestyle as fixed or permanent. This mindset can lead to many traps.

Does this mean I should sell my house and live in the middle of the woods?

No. If you own a home, God may call you to stay where you are in a crisis and become a place of ministry and refuge for family, friends, neighbors or other folks in need.

What about moving to a foreign country?

Everyone should have a passport. This is a form of liquidity. Further, knowledge of a second language becomes extremely important and a great asset if God is calling you to relocate. I am not an advocate of fleeing during a crisis; however, remember that God's people, relocating here and seeking freedom from religious persecution, were some of the earliest settlers in what is now the United States.

God may call some to relocate to other nations to help and support others who are suffering. It is good to be prepared and have knowledge about other options.

What about job skills and liquidity?

Transferable job skills are another high form of liquidity. Are you capable of earning a living in ways other than your current career? Could you earn a living in a foreign country with your present training? This is a very important asset to consider.

Should I allow my house to be foreclosed upon to be more liquid?

No. Our strategies should always demonstrate integrity and character and seek to honor God.

What about our spiritual condition? What is the best preparation for a crisis?

In Hebrews 10 we are told of Christians who were able to "joyfully" accept the confiscation of their property because they knew they had "better and lasting possessions." If that's your heart attitude, you are ready for any problem of biblical proportions.

Do you think that it could come to the point, for example, if somebody has a mortgage, the government comes in and says, "Pay it all now or we will take your home from you?"

The current trend is that the government is going to own or control all the mortgages in our country soon. That would put the government in a position to call everyone's note and make everybody a tenant of the government. It would be an unlikely move and not one I would lose sleep over. However, the Bible warns that the borrower is servant to the lender.

The Enemy never lets a good crisis go to waste. What kind of chaos do you think Christians can expect?

The Enemy always takes new ground, new territory when there's chaos. And, in fact, the evidence of this is in Matthew 24. When people are suffering, there will be deceivers who say, "Jesus is over here. Jesus is out here. Jesus is this. Jesus is that." And they're going to be trying to recruit the gullible, vulnerable people who are not grounded in truth. There will be confusion and persecution at intense levels.

I think Christians are unprepared for the tables turning against us in this culture. One day we will be outcasts in our society. It has happened in many other countries and I think we've got to prepare people to realize that deception spreads during events like this. Even in the Babylonian exile in Jeremiah 29, there were false prophets in among the people of God. And God sent a prophet to tell them, "Stop listening to them." We must be watchful of false prophets in a crisis.

What about fraud and financial scams during a crisis?

People are more vulnerable to financial fraud when times are tough. Criminals ratchet up scams that give people false hope when they are weak. I think we'll see a lot fraud in the days ahead. So be vigilant for financial schemes. If it seems to good to be true, it probably is.

What is the difference between a survivalist plan and The S.A.L.T. Plan?

The enemy desires for it to get darker, not lighter. My concern is that if Christians aren't strong enough, we could, in a major crisis, collapse into a modern Dark Age where the church gets weak and "unsalty." But if we're prepared, Christians can shine the brightest in that darkness. If we live God's way, it will be our finest hour, not our worst.

Christians will either have a survivalist mentality or a sacrificing mentality. In the crisis we will know the wheat from the chaff, the sheep from the goats. The goat will go into a survivalist mode; the sheep will go into a self-sacrificing mode. The faithful Christian will say, "Everything I have belongs to God. Everything I've prepared for is for the benefit of those God has called me to serve."

We are not to be little house plants that are comfortable and unprepared for a storm, because the storms will come. It rains on the righteous and the unrighteous. The truth has to be already embedded in our hearts to be exercised and lived out serving other people. When the survivalist mentality grows exponentially in the culture, the love and sacrificing mentality must increase in the Christian. *"Greater love has no one than this, that he lay down his life for his friends."*

Do you think America could become a nation where Christians are persecuted and suffer for His sake?

Yes. I think many Christians view church like a community activity or a club. Something is wrong when you have more people attending church than any time since the country began, but every year fewer people say they believe that the Bible is true. This trend is like rot under the bark of a tree, making it unprepared to stand during a storm.

In England today, if you are a Bible-believing Christian, you are considered stupid and intolerant. You are likely to suffer scorn from the intellectual community. In America, more and more Christians are called "haters." That is calling good evil and evil good. But that's what happens when the culture no longer believes the Bible is the infallible standard of truth.

Is something epic likely to occur within the next decade?

No man knows the future, but we can all see danger coming. I believe we need to be ready regardless of the timing.

ABOUT CROWN

Crown's vision is to see the followers of Christ in every nation faithfully living by God's financial principles in every area of their life so they are free to serve Him more fully. As an interdenominational Christian ministry, Crown serves people seeking to improve their personal finances, businesses and careers.

Crown employs a variety of media, including dramatic films, video, radio, podcasts, seminars and small group studies to achieve this end. Our mission is accomplished through a global network of dedicated staff and volunteers.

Founded in 1976, Crown Financial Ministries is a 501(c)(3) nonprofit educational organization. Headquartered in the suburbs of Atlanta, Georgia, Crown has operations in cities across the United States and is active on five continents.

We invite you to get acquainted with us. It is our privilege to serve you.

Crown.org

ABOUT CHUCK BENTLEY

For over a decade, Chuck Bentley has traveled the world teaching biblical financial principles to the affluent, middle class, poor and ultra poor. As host of the daily national radio broadcast, *My MoneyLife*™, Chuck connects with all generations and inspires his audience with a strong scriptural emphasis.

Following in the footsteps of Crown's cofounders, Howard Dayton and the late Larry Burkett, Chuck leads Crown Financial Ministries, an organization founded in the Atlanta area in 1976 that now reaches around the world with staff or volunteers on every continent.

Chuck is author of *The Root of Riches: What if Everything You Think about Money Is Wrong?* and he is the executive producer of the *God Provides*™ *Film Learning Experience*, Crown's first series of short films. He is also the co-creator of the *Crown Money Map*™ and a contributor to Saddleback Church's small group series, *Managing Our Finances God's Way.* These powerful resources are being used to transform lives around the world.

A Texas native, Chuck is a graduate of Baylor University, where he earned a bachelor's degree in Business Administration. He is a frequent speaker on biblical financial topics at church and business functions.

Chuck and his wife, Ann, were married in 1978. They live near Atlanta, Georgia and have four sons, a daughter-in-law, and a grandson. Chuck enjoys reading, the outdoors and spending time with his family.

You can stay in touch with Chuck, follow his blog, join Facebook and Twitter and be a part of the global Crown community—all at Crown.org.